WILD SOUTH

WILD SOUTH

Saving New Zealand's Endangered Birds

ROD MORRIS ♦ HAL SMITH

FOREWORD BY
Sir David Attenborough

TVNZ
in association with
Century Hutchinson

First published 1988 by
TVNZ
in association with
Century Hutchinson NZ Ltd
PO Box 40086 Auckland 10
ISBN 0-908690-38-X

Typeset by Wordset Enterprises Limited, Wellington
Printed by Everbest Printing Co. Ltd, Hong Kong
Design by Missen & Geard Ltd

During the ten years of research and filming for the *Wild South* programmes on which the chapters of this book are based, we have had the help of many talented people. They have generously given their specialist knowledge, their time, practical assistance in the field and have been good companions.

We especially wish to acknowledge the Wildlife Service who welcomed us on many of their most difficult assignments, resulting in some of our best documentaries. This book recognises the enormous debt we owe the New Zealand Wildlife Service which handed its responsibilities over to the new Department of Conservation in March 1987.

Many individuals generously contributed their experiences and advised on particular chapters in this book. In addition to those already mentioned in the text, we would like to thank Athol Anderson, Lexie Arnott, Cathie Brumley, Richard Holdaway, Dick Jackson, Euan Kennedy, Lionel and Jean Lobb, Alan Mark, Chris Robertson, Rodney Russ, Stan Sharpe and Tony Trotter.

Charles Fleming kindly read the entire manuscript and saved us from many mistakes.

Acknowledgement is also due to our colleagues in the Natural History Unit of Television New Zealand who provided many of the anecdotes recounted in the book. In particular Bev and Robert Brown, Paul Donovan, Neil Harraway, Peter Hayden, Mike Lemmon and Errol Samuelson.

We thank Neil Rowe, TVNZ's and now *The Listener*'s Publishing Manager, for patiently overseeing the book through its long and chequered history.

Finally, we have to thank a remarkable editor, Jane Thomson, for her contributions to the content, shape and clarity of the text.

To Mertie

Contents

Foreword

Of Birds and Men

ON A SMALL NEW ZEALAND ISLAND there once lived a species of tiny wren. For many years no one knew of the existence of the small, secretive birds until a lighthouse was built on the island in 1894 and a lighthouse keeper went to live there. He took his pet cat to keep him company. While the lighthouse keeper worked in the lighthouse the cat explored the new island. Within days the cat discovered the wrens.

When the lighthouse keeper himself saw the first of the birds it was already dead. His cat had brought it back to the lighthouse. Several nights later the lighthouse keeper saw three of the birds running like mice among the rocks in search of food, as he took his evening walk. They puzzled him and so he sent the body of the dead wren to a scientist in Wellington. Later the tiny bird was sent on to London. It appeared to be one of the most ancient birds living in New Zealand, and was perhaps the smallest flightless bird in the world.

Back on the island, the lighthouse keeper continued to find more dead wrens. Each killed by the cat. When ornithologists at last arrived on the island to learn more about the wren and how it lived, it was too late. No more were ever found. Only the cat knew how many wrens once lived on the island.

"The Lighthouse Keeper's Cat" is a true story told in schools throughout New Zealand. It is a parable of the land — the story of New Zealand's natural history in miniature. The archipelago of islands which make up New Zealand was filled with fantastic birds for millenia. It was a land of opportunity, but the only creatures to take advantage of its rich plant life and variety of landscapes were birds, which evolved in remarkable ways, occupying ecological niches filled by mammals elsewhere — there were birds like mice, birds like hedgehogs, like squirrels, like giraffes. Then man came with his predatory animals and wiped out whole species — sometimes with amazing speed, especially during the last century. They did not all go as quickly as the mouse-like wren on tiny Stephens Island. Still at least fifty percent of New Zealand's land birds have become extinct in the one thousand years since man first arrived. Eighteen species or subspecies have disappeared in the last 140 years and a further 60 are now rare or are threatened with extinction — more than in any other country in the world.

Among the first to disappear was one of the most spectacular, the moa. I first learned of this astonishing bird when, as a small boy, I started reading about records and superlatives and I discovered, with amazement, that one species of moa stood over nine feet high and was the tallest bird that ever existed. I still remember my bitter disappointment when I also found out that it was dead and gone and that I would never see it. At

David Attenborough with reconstructed Dinornis *skeleton.* Photo Ned Kelly, courtesy Otago Museum the time, I accounted for its extinction by bundling it together in my mind with dinosaurs and other prehistoric beasts long since vanished from the earth. It was only later that I learned that the moa had not lived tens of millions of years ago alongside the brontosaurus, but had been alive within the last few centuries — and that men had been responsible for its destruction.

As I became a little more knowledgeable about natural history and read more about New Zealand's extraordinary birds, so I became more and more eager to visit the islands. Half a life-time later, I managed to do so. I inspected the sites of the moa-hunters' settlements and looked at the skeletons of a whole range of moa species, small and large. I spent days sitting in the forests watching tuis and fantails. Most thrilling of all, I saw the kakapo.

This bird, arguably, is even more extraordinary than the moa itself. After all, the diminutive cousin of the moa, the kiwi, still survives, and elsewhere in the world there are cassowaries and ostriches that can give us a vivid idea of the appearance and character of the vanished moa. But nothing can quite prepare you for the kakapo. It is a giant parrot that has become flightless. Its feathers are moss-green and almost furry in texture, and it runs along trails it has cleared through the bush, cropping leaves, like a rabbit. A few that still survive have now been gathered together on Little Barrier Island off the coast of the North Island. One or two have been fitted with tiny radio transmitters so that their whereabouts and welfare can be monitored. At the time of my visit, one of them needed its battery replaced. I helped and in the process had the privilege of holding this solemn, gentle and extraordinarily endearing bird. As it sat peaceably in my arms, I wondered whether my grandchildren would read of the strange and wonderful kakapo with the same sadness and regret with which I had read about the moa, or whether they would still have the chance of seeing the living creature.

If the kakapo does survive, it will be due almost entirely to the efforts of Don Merton and his colleagues in the New Zealand Wildlife Service (now the Department of Conservation). Conservationists elsewhere in the world sometimes suppose that all that could or should be done to save a species is to build a fence around its habitat and rely on the endangered animal to look after itself. But on occasion, that is not enough. The New Zealand Wildlife Service, because of the urgency of the situation with which it was faced, decided to take a much more enterprising and active approach. They developed great skills in handling and translocating birds. With verve and imagination they devised ways of inducing birds to breed and of maximising their reproductive potential. Repeatedly, they managed to convert a few scattered individuals into thriving breeding populations.

These successes have brought the Service world-wide fame. Don Merton's expertise is sought after internationally. He was asked to use his skills in Australia, to save the Noisy Scrub Bird. He went to Mauritius to rescue the Echo Parakeet and to Christmas Island to prevent the extinction of Abbott's Booby.

The Service's achievements became known to other conservationists through specialist ornithological journals, but it was also shown to a vastly wider and more general audience through the medium of television. The remarkable films produced by the Broadcasting Corporation of New Zealand for the *Wild South* programme captured the attention and kindled the enthusiasm of millions of people world-wide. This book is an account of the experiences of those primarily responsible for those films. It is clear from what is written that they were far from being passive and detached observers during those expeditions. They too, cared passionately about the fate of these birds.

I believe the future will show that their help was not simply to give practical assistance in the field. In the end, birds like the kakapo and kiwi, the takahe and the yellow-eyed penguin will not survive unless people at large want them to do so. The *Wild South* films must have convinced millions of how precious these strange and beautiful birds are. Likewise, this book may well bring crucial sympathy and help to these imperilled creatures and to those who are working so devotedly and skilfully to save them. I know that its authors could have no greater hope for it.

Sir David Attenborough C.B.E., F.R.S.

Introduction

IN 1974, A YOUNG JOURNALIST with Television New Zealand in Dunedin persuaded his editor to allow him to take a news crew by helicopter into a remote alpine valley in the heart of Fiordland, to film a short item on the takahe. It was to cost no more than any other news story he said.

The takahe is a remarkable bird that had been rediscovered in 1948, and by the 1970s seemed once again on the verge of extinction. Permission for the trip was granted, provided the film crew were back in time for their next assignment.

Within half an hour of their arriving in the Chester Burn, cloud descended on the mountains and the weather deteriorated. The three-man crew remained stuck in the valley for seven days, at first in a small tent, and then, when that collapsed, crammed into a tiny two-man hut (later described as being too small for a dog kennel), along with three Wildlife Service officers.

In all that time the weather gave them no opportunity either to see or hear the mysterious takahe. However it did give them time to talk. On the seventh day the weather cleared enough for the helicopter to come in to return them to Dunedin — without their story. They did however take back the germ of an idea. The trip marked the very beginning of our Natural History Unit and was the starting point for the very first *Wild South* documentary, "Project Takahe".

The conversations which ran long into the night in that tiny mountain hut, gave birth to an idea which was to develop amongst the film crew and the men from the New Zealand Wildlife Service. At that time a number of birds on the verge of extinction were being rediscovered. New efforts were being made to try and save them. Dramas were being acted out in remote corners of this country, which were every bit as exciting as the wildlife programmes from overseas appearing on our television screens.

The potential for such stories interested two of the TV crew in particular — journalist Neil Harraway and cameraman Bob Brown. Both men had an interest in the outdoors that had been with them since childhood.

It wasn't long before the same crew made a second trip to film the takahe news story, and this time they were successful. They were again encouraged in their efforts by Jim Mills, the Wildlife Service takahe scientist. He told them that a kakapo had been found that same week by a Wildlife Service team under Don Merton, in a valley near Milford Sound. Here was an opportunity for another "rare bird" story. After a brief call to the Wildlife Service seeking official permission, they found themselves at dawn on a typically dark and gloomy Fiordland day in the Esperance Valley. They had to move quickly

Hut interior, Takahe workers' camp, Murchison Mountains, Fiordland. Photo Rod Morris

to be back in Dunedin that same day. To save time, the helicopter pilot landed as close to camp as he dared in the half light — at the foot of a waterfall.

The TV crew were taken to a dark little aviary, where Bob Brown crawled amongst the ferns and scrub, snatching just enough precious footage of the secretive kakapo to illustrate the story; then they were off back to Dunedin.

In the little time available, they had gathered enough material for a news story on the kakapo, and by carefully editing all the pieces together, they found they had enough left over for a six-minute item for the local news magazine programme. They did the same with the takahe story. It was in this way that longer and longer news items on local natural history subjects began appearing on New Zealand television. They were successful, and attracted much public interest.

The TV crew and the scientists whose work they were filming worked well together in the field. All were prepared to rough it in an effort to get unique footage never before seen on our screens. Much of Bob Brown's success lay in his keen interest in wildlife, and ability to observe quietly for long periods of time to get the film or information needed. The notion of a TV unit comprising people interested in natural history grew. It wasn't a new idea. The BBC already had such a Unit up and running — perhaps the New Zealand Unit could be modelled on that.

Wildlife officers working in remote areas, in particular Jim Mills and Don Merton, were enthusiastic about their work being seen by large television audiences. In this way they felt more New Zealanders would come to share in the growing concern for our threatened wildlife.

Jim and Don took their ideas back to the Wildlife Service Head Office, and discussed them there, while Bob Brown and Neil Harraway began discussions within television.

Fortunately, at about that time, the formation of a Unit like the BBC's Natural History Unit was proposed quite independently by Dunedin's station manager Hal Weston, who had just visited the BBC and saw the potential in New Zealand for similar programmes.

Some doubt was expressed in both groups at first. The Wildlife Service was concerned that scientific work might be handicapped by the intrusion of film crews. Television New Zealand was worried that such programmes would be too difficult and expensive to make, and that large sums of money would be spent on risky expeditions to film creatures which were scarcely ever seen at all. There the matter rested for some time. It appeared as if there would be no Unit after all.

Then the Director of the Wildlife Service, Gordon Williams, wrote to Hal Weston. This was all that was needed. In 1977, the TVNZ Natural History Unit officially began.

Four people comprised the unit at first — two directors, Neil Harraway and Robin Scholes; a cameraman, Bob Brown; and a producer, Graeme Wilson. Amongst them, these four had the necessary skills to make the first wildlife programmes. With the variety of skills they shared, they were able to get the infant Unit functioning. After one short series Graeme and Robin left, and it seemed that the Unit was itself in danger. Then Michael Stedman became executive producer, the Unit stabilised and the first *Wild South*s began to appear.

Sound men and film editors were drawn in from the station whenever they were needed at first and new people joined the unit. Sound man Errol Samuelson's work was increasingly relied upon, Peter Hayden became the Unit's narrator and scriptwriter and I left the Wildlife Service and became researcher and later director. Gradually others joined the Natural History Unit, sometimes as permanent members of the staff, sometimes drawn in for particular assignments.

Among those working for the Unit there was soon a tremendous enthusiasm and energy for the work. At planning sessions, ideas flew around the table, changing shape and growing until they were unrecognisable to the originator. The Unit seemed to develop a momentum of its own.

Earlier on, we had written to Christopher Parsons, head of the BBC Natural History Unit, to tell him that the New Zealand Unit had been set up. Chris wrote back encouraging us to keep in touch, and to send copies of programmes for him to look at. He also advised that it would probably be simplest to begin with the more common animals such as rabbits and deer, to try to give audiences an intimate view of their private lives.

This was a piece of advice we were slow to take. Already we were heading in a different direction. The 1970s were critical times for our own unique and rapidly disappearing wildlife. We wanted to use the resources we had to capture survivors from New Zealand's ancient past on film, before they had gone forever. When our first *Wild South* programmes were made, several of them were about endangered birds.

From the beginning, theirs seemed a more interesting story to tell. The longer we have gone on, the more that story has unfolded.

Rod Morris

Chapter One

Beginnings

TEN YEARS HAVE ELAPSED since we began filming *Wild South*. During one of the more recent programmes, we examined how many of the birds shown in earlier programmes have fitted into the whole extraordinary history of our land.

Entitled "The Land of the Kiwi" it was about the evolution of New Zealand, and was made in conjunction with the BBC Natural History Unit. Such joint projects demonstrate that the unique birds of New Zealand (30% of which are classified as endangered species) have aroused an interest which goes well beyond our shores.

It was about 86 million years ago that the land mass now known as New Zealand broke away from the vast southern continent which geologists call Gondwana. Through the gradual process of continental drift, New Zealand became isolated from any other land mass. It became a floating ark of strange, ancient life forms, descendants of which survive today. We filmed them to illustrate the story of the evolution of these islands.

The small new land carried primitive forests brought from the warm, fertile continent of Gondwana: these trees are the ancestors of those still growing in our forests. There were ferns which grew as large as trees, like today's mamaku, or black tree fern; primitive cone-bearers, like the gigantic New Zealand kauri; podocarps like the totara, rimu and kahikatea; and forests of southern beech, like those in Fiordland today. Primitive flowering plants such as rewarewa, the New Zealand honeysuckle, were probably in the forest too. And there were trees which didn't survive, such as eucalypts and coconut palms. Only fossils of their leaves and fruits are left as clues to the history of the land.

Strange creatures flourished in the forest. There are few fossils to tell us what they were like, but some of their descendants live on as a living fossil record. One was peripatus — a curious little creature, popularly called the "missing link", described by a scriptwriter as being "half-way between a worm and an insect, that trundles on its inflated legs like a mobile barrage balloon." One of the most ancient creatures still in existence, its history goes back 500 million years. We also filmed wetas, giant spiky insects, amongst the heaviest in the world. They may have been in existence for 200 million years. From the same era come tiny primitive frogs, and giant carnivorous snails which smother and devour native worms which may themselves reach up to a metre in length. And there is a strange little dragon with a vestigial third eye, the tuatara — a primitive reptile, like those from which the dinosaurs were descended.

Tuatara. Photo Rod Morris

In spite of this odd relic of the pre-dinosaur era, the age of the great dinosaurs had probably passed when the land went to sea. The age of mammals had not yet begun, although two land mammals would arrive here later — both of them bats. One originated in South America and travelled here via the bridge of Antarctica, perhaps 40 million years ago, before the ocean gap became too wide. The second bat arrived more recently from Australia. However, in this small isolated land, birds, the feathered descendants of the age of reptiles, became the inheritors of the kingdom. Instead of being dominated by mammals, like most of the rest of the world in this era, New Zealand would evolve as a land of birds.

What birds came with New Zealand as it left Gondwana? This is something we cannot know, as there are no fossils to tell us. We do know that the ancestors of the kiwi and moa must have been here. Their bone and feather structure show that they belong to the very primitive group of ratite birds, which were probably flightless before Gondwana began breaking up. Unless the primitive ancestors of the moa and kiwi were still able to fly later than the Cretaceous period, the only way they could have got here was by walking. Kiwis are living examples of the very first birds which existed here. Yet we know that their ancestors, eighty million years ago, probably looked very different from the birds we see today. It seems that the kiwi was once a much larger bird, more like its cousin the moa, which gradually evolved as a small nocturnal forager — to fill an ecological niche occupied by mammals in other lands.

We also filmed penguin fossils, as New Zealand has the oldest penguin fossils in the world. (More fossil penguins have been found here than in any other region — sixteen of the thirty-two known fossil species.) The evidence suggests that the world's penguins originated in New Zealand's seas. However, if the ancestors of these birds were here eighty million years ago, they would have been unrecognisable and were probably flying birds. We know from fossil records that it was only about sixty-five million years ago that penguins, albatrosses and shearwaters evolved from the same ancient flying stock.

We were also able to film survivors of three families of birds unique to New Zealand and so primitive that their ancestors must have been here either before we broke away from Gondwana, or else came here very shortly afterwards. These are the New Zealand wrens, thrushes and wattlebirds. The New Zealand "wrens" are among the most primitive flying birds known. One species, the rifleman, is the tiniest bird existing in New Zealand today. Once there were two species of New Zealand thrush or piopio, not a true thrush, perhaps a kind of bower bird, although as they are now extinct we shall never know this for certain. There were also three species of wattlebirds — huia, saddleback and kokako, of these only two species still exist. All of these birds are different from any found elsewhere in the world.

New Zealand has many other strange and fascinating birds, which although related to birds in other lands, have evolved in peculiar ways. It is possible that some of them were here from the beginning, as many existing families of birds had already evolved by the time New Zealand was cast adrift. More probably the ancestors of these birds flew here millenia ago, colonising New Zealand. Gradually, the effects of living in a peaceful and

Peripatus. Photo Rod Morris

plenteous land, where there were no mammals to hunt them or eat their food, changed these birds. Many species lost the power of flight, as there was little need to fly. They came to nest and feed on or near the ground, in places where there was no protection from later introduced ground predators. They also had a tendency to become very large in size.

Amongst these birds are the parrots, which may have come here as small birds blown in on the winds. These have evolved into the kea, kaka, and the heavy flightless kakapo. There were robins and stilts, which probably arrived as brightly coloured or piebald birds, but which later developed a glossy blackness. The flying wetland birds, such as the rails, evolved here into the flightless weka and takahe; plovers, such as the wrybill which became the only bird in the world to have a beak bent to one side, enabling it to quickly pick up food organisms from under stones; honey-eaters evolved into the tui, bellbird and stitchbird, drinking nectar from the growing number of flowering plants appearing in the forests (from seeds blown by the wind or carried in by other birds); ducks of all kinds, such as the blue duck which still swims in swift mountain streams in undisturbed corners of New Zealand and searches for food with a sensitive white bill which blushes pink when the bird is surprised. And there are many other families of birds which stayed to develop peculiarly New Zealand characteristics.

Many of these birds can still be found, even if only in very small numbers. But there are many more which have gone, which are now known only through lifeless records.

There was the laughing owl — a bird with a maniacal scream, and long strong legs for running down its prey. Although it could fly it was well on its way to becoming flightless before it died out about 1914. There were birds which flew here from the northern hemisphere such as a sea-duck with a saw-toothed bill (a Merganser) also now extinct.

In fact, the more we learned of the times when New Zealand was a kingdom of birds, the more we wished we could have seen the bizarre and beautiful creatures which must once have lived here.

For "The Land of the Kiwi" we did come closer to seeing some of the birds which have vanished than had ever been possible before. It was in the Honeycomb Hill caves in Karamea on the West Coast of the South Island where there is a network of thirteen kilometres of cave passages, with more than seventy entrances open to the sky. Over the centuries many birds have fallen into the holes, been trapped in the caves and died there. Protected from the weather, their bones have been preserved, so that it is possible for palaeontologists to find out about birds which no one ever knew existed. It is a way of going back to a time thousands of years ago.

Our guide was an expert on sub-fossil bones, Trevor Worthy — a caver and zoologist who is delving deep into New Zealand's ancient past. He has not only been working in the Honeycomb Hill caves, but on sub-fossil bone deposits all over New Zealand and has developed a broad understanding of how the land used to be.

The picture Trevor painted for us was of a land alive with birds. Birds which had been thought to be restricted to one tiny habitat, such as the extinct Stephens Island wren, once lived all over the North and South Islands. Birds which are very rare and special-

Male Rifleman. Photo Rod Morris

Following page *Giant treeferns, Whirinaki.* Photo Rod Morris

ised, such as the takahe, kakapo, kokako, snipe, and many others, were found in a variety of habitats from North Cape to Bluff. As well as the terrestrial birds, there were vast numbers of oceanic birds such as petrels and shearwaters — as Trevor said, "These sea birds used to nest inland over the length and breadth of the land."

Perhaps the most exciting part of this work has been the discovery of long-extinct birds. Trevor's own interest had originally been the very small birds — long neglected in favour of the larger moa. Small bird remains were abundant in caves, and their study revealed just how fascinating our fauna used to be. He gave us an account of the group of primitive wrens in which new discoveries have shown how these birds had adapted to fit various conditions as New Zealand changed. The tiny fragments of their bones found in the Honeycomb Hill caves have been put together to uncover new secrets. He said:

One was a small bird about the size of a sparrow. But in comparison with a sparrow, its legs were built like those of a moa — they were extremely stout and strong. It obviously couldn't fly, because its wing bones were small spindly things. It may have been one of the smallest flightless birds ever known. And recently the skeleton of another kind of wren has been found with a great long curving bill, rather like that of a huia.

At the opposite end of the scale, he had also become increasingly interested in the way our most famous extinct bird, the giant moa, had adapted in various ways to fit differing conditions. In fact, it is quite misleading to talk about "the moa". For a long time it has been known that there were many species of moa — probably about twelve. As better skeletons are found it is being realised just how different each species was. Some were quite small, others were huge. Some were long-legged and swift runners, others were very heavy and slow, with short thick-set legs. They also had slightly different beaks. A few were strongly curved downwards and would have cut like secateurs; most were more-or-less straight; but it shows that they must have eaten different kinds of food. The bird which we usually think of as "the moa", *Dinornis maximus,* was just one of a dozen varieties of the bird.

Trevor also told of other fabulous extinct birds: of giant geese, pelicans and native swans; of a giant penguin from an even earlier period, now found only in fossil form, which stood as tall as a man; and of a giant rail, about twice as heavy as a takahe, which stood about a metre high and had a beak fifteen centimetres long, rather like a woodpecker's beak. But the most spectacular extinct bird Trevor introduced us to was truly extraordinary — a giant eagle.

Before he told the story, he took the film crew to a passage known as "the eagle's roost". As in so many caves in the Honeycomb Hill, the entrance or tomo was a death trap — a deep shaft cutting down through the limestone, open to the forest and the sky high overhead. Standing amongst the moss-strewn boulders and broken moa bones on the floor of the dripping wet shaft, looking up at the sky, was like being at the bottom of a gigantic well. Some time in the distant past, two giant eagles had swooped down into the dim, green well, probably to feed on dead and dying moas which had fallen into the hole. The eagles in turn were trapped. On a small dry ledge above the scattered bones of

Extinct Merganser. Photo Rod Morris, courtesy Otago Museum

their prey lay two perfect skeletons of the giant eagle, *Harpagornis*.

The great birds must have weighed about twelve kilograms, and had a wing span of 2·5 metres, perhaps the heaviest eagle ever to exist. There are Maori legends of a terror bird, which used to fly down from the mountains and snatch up people. Europeans once treated such stories as myth but the New Zealand eagle may well have been the realistic basis of these stories. It was certainly large enough to kill even the largest moa. To see its skeleton is to glimpse a strange lost world.

In our documentary human beings didn't come into the picture. This was a programme about the land and its plants and wildlife over millions of years. Man is a recent arrival. However in most of the *Wild South* programmes made by our Natural History Unit, human beings are very much part of the story. In recent times, it is the human element which has disrupted the ancient world of the birds, created the difficult conditions they now face, and turned them into endangered species.

It was probably not much more than a thousand years ago that the vast moat of ocean that surrounds these islands was bridged by large double canoes, and the mammal which had long been dominant elsewhere finally reached New Zealand. This land was trodden for the first time by human feet. Anthropologists think that the first arrivals came from somewhere in East Polynesia, bringing with them taro, gourds and kumara, together with the food dog kuri and food rat kiore. Because there wasn't the same scope for horticulture here that there was in their warmer homelands they quickly adapted to reaping the riches of the birdlife they found, eating many of the larger and meatier birds and using their skins and feathers for clothes or decoration. They also cut down forest trees for canoes and houses, and cleared some areas by fire for agriculture. Their rats and dogs ate birds' eggs and chicks.

Suddenly the birds of this land had powerful predators and competitors. The Maori were a people with a deep and abiding regard for nature. They revered the dense forests filled with birdsong. They came to think of the trees and birds as their distant kin — children of the god Tane like themselves. Yet, despite this, their entry into this fragile environment had a devastating effect over a thousand years.

However, it was the immigration of people from Britain and Western Europe less than two centuries ago that brought the most dramatic changes. The new settlers came well-armed and determined to turn this strange country into a replica of the long-tamed lands they'd left behind them. With fire and axes, they destroyed huge areas of dense forest. With guns they shot the many birds they found — for sport, curiosity or food. They introduced rabbits, deer and goats to provide more sport and food for themselves, and these animals were soon competing with browsing birds for food. The rabbits multiplied so quickly that they became a plague to farmers, and so ferrets, stoats and weasels were introduced as a means of rabbit control. By this time, Norway rats, black rats and wild cats were also running loose in the countryside. It took less than fifty years for the European colonists to unleash the major predatory mammals we are cursed with today. Suddenly the birds, which had had the land to themselves for so long, were

Laughing Owl. Photo Rod Morris, courtesy Otago Museum

Following page *Moa skeleton, Honeycomb Cave*. Photo Rod Morris

surrounded by new and dangerous enemies.

Soon the terrible effects on bird life became apparent. Some species completely disappeared. Others were becoming very rare. A growing number of people — scientists and laymen alike — were extremely concerned about what was happening. It appeared that the ancient heritage of this land, much of it found nowhere else on earth, was being recklessly destroyed. During the 1870s and 1880s a few lone voices of protest were raised. Around the turn of the century one or two bird sanctuaries were set up, and eventually legal protection was given to some native birds.

During the twentieth century, the government became more involved in trying to organise the protection of native species, setting up a Wildlife Branch of the Internal Affairs Department in 1947. At first they worked mainly at trying to control deer and predators. Then a more effective Wildlife Act was passed in 1953, which provided for government protection and management of native species, and scientists were employed to advise wildlife managers. In the 1960s and 1970s groups of people were beginning to work in remote areas, trying to save some of our more remarkable birds from disappearing forever. There was a growing conservation movement in the community at this time, and an increasing number of people were anxious to support the work of the Wildlife officers and scientists. This was the climate in which the Natural History Unit began.

The birds which these people were trying to save were the stars of our first *Wild South* programmes, but one or two people became part of that story too. Always there was far too much fascinating material to fit into the short space of a television programme. In this book we've tried to record a little more of what we've learned and some of the experiences we've been privileged to have had while making *Wild South* programmes.

There have also been far too many subjects to crowd into our limited schedule. Many ideas have been suggested for programmes which have not yet been made — about birds which are endangered, birds which are still flourishing, and birds which have become extinct. There is an abundance and variety of subject matter which we have only begun to explore. In the next chapter we look at four birds which have so far just been glimpsed briefly in *Wild South* programmes yet each enjoys a special place in our national imagination, and each has a story which illustrates in a different way the impact of humankind on New Zealand's bird life.

Quintin Mackinnon (standing) in camp with two dead blue ducks (hanging from ridgepole and his belt) and captive kakapo. Photo Fred Muir (1888), courtesy Hocken Library

Previous page

A Victorian collection of remarkable New Zealand birds including a yellow kea, a red kaka, white kaka and yellow kakapo. Photo Rod Morris, courtesy Canterbury Museum

Chapter Two

Brief Encounters

Huia

The Magical Bird

THE LENS TRACKED SLOWLY along a graceful ivory-coloured arc, lit against a background of darkness. It was the beak of a female huia — perhaps one of New Zealand's most remarkable birds.

The cameraman remembers: "I tried to light it as glamorously as I could, because it was such a magical bird." But he felt sadness for a magic which had probably passed away. The huia he was filming was a museum specimen, preserved by the taxidermist's art. The last authenticated sighting of a huia, now generally accepted as extinct, was in 1907.

The film of the huia was just part of the supporting material for a programme on another subject. Yet perhaps it brought the huia back to life in people's minds for a moment. We hoped the image would arouse the same kinds of questions in others' minds as it had in ours. Why had such a beautiful bird become extinct? What was its story?

The huia was one of New Zealand's ancient wattle-birds, probably dating back to the era before this land was separated from Gondwana. It was the only bird in the world to have had a totally differently-shaped bill for male and female — the male's shorter, stouter bill being used for hammering rotten logs apart, while the female's long slender bill was used to probe into the deep hiding-places of the large huhu grubs and insects which were the huia's favoured food. Old-timers maintained that pairs hunted together in life-long partnership, and Sir Walter Buller wrote:

Sometimes I observed the male remove the decayed portion without being able to reach the grub, when the female would at once come to his aid, and accomplish with her long slender bill what he had failed to do. I noticed however that the female always appropriated to her own use the morsels thus obtained.

Another of the huia's remarkable features was its long glossy-black tail feathers, each one tipped with a broad band of white. The tail was often spread to help the bird

Female huia. Photo Rod Morris, courtesy Otago Museum

balance, as it clung vertically to rotting tree trunks. As Buller also wrote:

It was most interesting to watch these graceful birds hopping from branch to branch, occasionally spreading the tail into a broad fan, displaying themselves in a variety of natural attitudes and then meeting to caress each other with their ivory bills, uttering at the same time a low affectionate twitter.

To the Maori, the huia was *tapu* — sacred above all other birds of the forest. A sign of the greatest chiefly rank was to wear its white-tipped tail feathers. Although the huia was found only in the North Island, particularly in the dense forested hills and steep valleys of the Tararua, Ruahine, Rimutaka and Kaimanawa ranges, its tail feathers were worn by people of rank all over the land. They were presented from tribe to tribe as signs of great honour and kept in waka huia — intricately-carved wooden boxes hung from the roof beams of chiefs' houses.

Huia were killed by Maori hunters for their feathers, but only in limited numbers. The threats to their existence did not come until Europeans arrived.

Some of these new dangers were common to most native birds. There were the predators such as stoats and cats which attacked the huia as they hopped around the ground or looked for food low on tree trunks. Another major threat was the destruction of the ancient forests in which they lived. Only mature forests provided the rotting trees in which the huia found huhu grubs. Second-growth forest, however flourishing, could not give them a home. The disappearance of the bush before the advancing tide of pakeha settlement left them few places in which to live. Still, the huia survived in the densely-wooded hill-tops which constituted a permanent forest reserve.

There were yet other factors threatening the huia — exceptional ones caused by its striking beauty. It was a large bird, with glossy green-black plumage, and waxy-orange wattles each as big and round as a penny clinging to the underside of its chin. The European settlers were not indifferent to the huia. Unfortunately many thought of exploiting its beauty for financial gain. Bird enthusiasts were aware that every museum and collector in the world would like a showcase containing the bird with the orange-petalled face and the beautifully arching beak. Several thousand huia swiftly found their way to taxidermists' benches in every quarter of the globe. The plunder had begun.

The huia was by no means a difficult bird to destroy. It was quiet and curious and unaccustomed to enemies. Ernst Dieffenbach described an experience in the 1840s:

From the hills surrounding Port Nicholson, I added to my collection a very curious bird. . . . Accompanied by a native . . . I set out for the hills, and, after a long day's walk, had the pleasure of seeing that the continued loud and shrill whistling of my guide, uia, uia, uia, *in imitation of the note of the birds, had attracted four, which alighted on the lower branches of the trees near him. They came silently and with a brisk flight. I fired and killed two or three of them. . . .*

Sir Walter Buller described a number of similar experiences, which seem especially interesting in that he was a man with a deep love of birds, having grown up (as the son of a missionary) in New Zealand before it was touched much by the effects of settlement. As a boy he became interested in the creatures around him, and grew up to be the most

Waka huia. *Photo Rod Morris, courtesy Otago Museum*

noted New Zealand ornithologist of his day. Yet he showed his love of the birds in a typically Victorian way by collecting large numbers of dead ones, as well as observing them in life.

In 1867, he was in the Ruahine Ranges:

We heard the soft flute-note of the Huia in the wooded gully far beneath us. One of our native companions at once imitated the call, and in a few seconds a pair of beautiful Huias, male and female, appeared in the branches near us. They remained gazing at us only a few instants, and then started off up the side of the hill, moving by a succession of hops, often along the ground, the male generally leading. Waiting until he could get both birds in a line, my friend at length pulled trigger. . . .

In 1883, he described several such incidents in the Tararua Ranges:

In a few seconds, without sound or warning of any kind, a Huia came bounding along, almost tumbling, through the close foliage of the pukapuka, and presented himself to view at such close range that it was impossible to fire. This gave me an opportunity of watching this beautiful bird and marking his noble bearing, if I may so express it, before I shot him . . .

My next shot was at an adult male Huia who came dashing up, with reckless impetuosity, from the wooded gully. Being anxious to obtain a perfect specimen, I risked a long shot and only wounded my bird. Down he went to the ground like an arrow, with a sharp flute-note of surprise or pain, and then darted off, kangaroo-fashion, covering the ground with wonderful rapidity, and disappeared in the tangle. . . .

A pair of Huias, without uttering a sound, appeared in a tree overhead, and as they were caressing each other with their beautiful bills, a charge of No. 6 brought both to ground together. The incident was rather touching, and I felt almost glad that the shot was not mine, although by no means loth to appropriate the two fine specimens.

Perhaps Buller's most extraordinary description was a few years later, when he casually shot a huia, even though he was well aware that the birds were becoming rare:

To show how much scarcer this bird is than it was formerly, I may mention that in 1892, accompanied by Mr Morgan Carkeek, I made an expedition into the wooded ranges at the back of Waikanae. . . . During the whole expedition we only saw a single Huia — which I shot — a male bird, which visited our camp in the early morning. Mr Carkeek assures me that when exploring and surveying in these ranges only five or six years before the Huia was comparatively plentiful.

By this time, many people were realising that too many of the beautiful birds had been killed. Huia were generally becoming very hard to find. Maori people were the first to become concerned about the decline of their sacred bird. In the 1880s, chiefs in the Manawatu and Wairarapa began a movement to try to save them. They placed a tapu on the Tararua Range, saying that no more huia were to be killed there. In 1892, when the Earl of Onslow, then Governor of New Zealand, asked an assembly of Maori chiefs for a name for his newly-born son, they asked him to call the boy "Huia", and one said:

There, yonder, is the snow-clad Ruahine Range, the home of our favourite bird. We ask you, O

Gottfried Lindauer, 1878, Tukukino of Ngati Maru. *Partridge Collection, Auckland City Art Gallery.*

Lindauer 1878

Governor! to restrain the pakeha from shooting it, that when your boy grows up he may see the beautiful bird which bears his name.

The Earl of Onslow, one of the most remarkable Governors in New Zealand history, responded to this call. An ardent conservationist and lover of nature, he was deeply concerned with the protection of this country's unique bird life and began the first official attempts to try to stop its destruction. It was through his influence that in 1892, the government issued an edict that no huia was to be taken in any part of New Zealand. Throughout the 1890s, sanctuary islands were established — Resolution Island in Dusky Sound, Little Barrier Island in the Hauraki Gulf, Kapiti Island near Wellington, and Motu Ngaro Island in the Marlborough Sounds — sanctuaries which are still vital today.

Unfortunately, none of the schemes for transferring huia to island sanctuaries even got underway. They broke down in bickering amongst government departments. It was improbable anyway that the shift would have been successful: by this time the islands were not totally free from the mammalian predators which infested the rest of the country.

In any case, before anything effective could be done to save the huia, they were dealt yet another blow. In 1901, the Duke and Duchess of York (the future King George V and Queen Mary) visited New Zealand. It was an event which caused the most lavish celebrations throughout the land. While the Royal couple were in Rotorua, they were given an official Maori welcome. A high-ranking Maori woman, a guide, took a huia feather from her hair and placed it in the band of the Duke's hat, showing that he was regarded as being a great chief.

It was a graceful gesture which caught the colonial imagination. But it was disastrous for the huia. Soon many people in New Zealand and in England wanted to follow the royal fashion and wear huia feathers in their hats. The price of tail feathers soared to £1 for a single feather, and some even went as high as £5. Under this relentless commercial pressure, the chiefly tapu and governmental edict against killing huia were forgotten. There was a last-ditch attempt at invoking government protection to save the huia, but it foundered on legal rocks in 1903 when the Solicitor-General ruled that there was no law to protect feathers.

The last "official" sighting of the huia was on December 28th, 1907. After that it was pronounced extinct — although perhaps its extinction was not quite as early as that. There were lingering reports of sightings of huia in the years that followed. The most consistent appear to have come from behind York Bay near Wellington. One was as late as December 12, 1922. A man familiar with the huia reported that he had once again been watching three huia in the Gollans Valley. (He had previously seen them there, and there had been other reports of huia being sighted in this area in 1840, 1855, 1864, 1894, 1912 and 1913.) It was well within the known range of the bird. Unfortunately no one at the museum took the trouble to go out and see!

Huia. Photo Rod Morris, courtesy Otago Museum

Moa

The Big Bird

IN 1983 THE BBC INVITED THE UNIT to join them in making an hour-long television special about the world's flightless birds. As most people think of birds as being flying creatures, the programme was to be called "Birds of Paradox".

Apart from holding something of a world record for endangered species, New Zealand is home to most of the world's remaining flightless birds. Of course we wanted to concentrate on filming the many which still exist here, but we also wanted to include the extinct moa, *Dinornis maximus*, once our largest and oldest flightless bird.

How do you create a vivid image of an extinct bird? We needed to place *Dinornis* back in the New Zealand landscape — somehow to bring it to life in the minds of viewers, and show its giant proportions in relation to a more familiar environment. So we embarked on a project which gave us more than a few headaches. Our director asked the Otago Museum if we could take one of their completely reconstructed moa skeletons out into the sort of environment it would once have occupied. There was understandable reluctance on their part. Still, after agreeing to careful supervision by Museum staff, we were permitted to remove an assembled tower of bone to the kind of country where it would once have walked in the flesh.

Current thinking is that *Dinornis* was something of a forest bird. It certainly doesn't appear to have been a tussock-eating bird as was once thought. The preserved contents of exhumed moa stomachs have shown that it ate seeds and berries, leaves, and a great amount of twigs and small branches from the lowland scrub. It ranged the fringes of the forests, feeding from trees it could reach with its tall neck like an avian giraffe. We therefore decided to take the moa skeleton to an area near Maclennan, 150 kilometres south of Dunedin, where the surrounding forest still contains pockets of ancient trees, like those which grew when moas walked the land.

It was a long and complex job, packing the sections of moa bones into crates, and taking them by truck to Maclennan. Here we lugged the heavy crates over the swampy ground to the edge of the forest, and the skeleton was re-assembled against the background of bush. Once assembled, the giant bird's skeleton stood taller than many of the surrounding trees and shrubs. The bird looked almost too big, too large to be real — or perhaps everything else has become too small. It made us realise New Zealand was once a place very different from what we know today. What must it have been like to see a live moa, roaming the forest fringe unchallenged, on legs as stout as saplings?

The only people to see the moa in all their might were the early Maori. Then the moas were lords of the land, and had been so for millions of years. They must have been a

Mummified moa head. Photo Rod Morris, courtesy British Museum of Natural History

spectacular feature of the landscape; twelve different species on these small isolated islands — a tremendous variety for any bird. They ranged from the smallest, about half a metre high (still large for a bird) to the huge *Dinornis maximus* which, standing erect, was about four metres high — the tallest bird known to humankind.

We have only fragments of information, small clues, to help us imagine what it might have been like to approach such birds. Archaeological evidence and oral tradition all help to build up a picture — or at least open our minds to the possibilities of what the moa might have been like.

Most people have an image of the moa as being a dull brown colour, largely because mock moas in museums are covered with feathers from kiwis and emus — the only birds in our part of the world to have the same kind of hair-like plumage. But was the moa really so drab? Moa feathers have been found with a variety of colours — brownish red, white on black, speckled grey and bluish purple. One of the Maori names for the bird is kuranui which implies that it had reddish-brown plumage. James Cowan, after talking to North Island Maori people in the nineteenth century, believed that the bird's feathers were usually grey. Perhaps the different species had plumage of different colours. The larger ones may well have had crests on their heads — as indicated by pits in their skulls. And perhaps, too, they had spectacularly-coloured patches of bare skin, as moa-like birds in other lands do, birds like the ostrich and cassowary. Did any of our moas have peacock-blue necks or pink legs? This is something we can never know — yet it seems likely that, with so many different species, they had coloured signals to locate mates of their own species at breeding time.

We cannot know either what kinds of calls the giant birds added to the chorus of sounds in the prehistoric forest. Did the air ring with the shriek of the moa? Herries Beattie collected many South Island Maori traditions about the bird, and one old informant told him that the bird had a "shrill sound, quite out of keeping with the size of the bird." Yet others told him of moa roars and booms. No doubt the different species of moa had a wide range of cries which sounded through the land.

One thing we do know for certain is that the moa was a forest browsing bird, eating leaves and twigs which it ground up in its gizzard. Botanists are now beginning to speculate about the effects millions of years of moa-browsing may have had on our forest structure. The birds must have been enormous eaters of plant food over the millenia. It seems that some of our plant forms might have developed as a kind of defence against their powerful beaks (just as plants in other lands have developed thorns to defend themselves against soft mammalian mouths). We have a higher proportion of divaricating plants in New Zealand than anywhere else in the world — plants which have a springy interlacing network of small outer branches, (ideal for keeping beaks away from the small leaves and berries growing inside). There are also a number of trees in New Zealand which have a divaricating juvenile form, lasting until they are about four metres high, when they develop a lusher, leafier foliage. Scientists now wonder if the plants developed these forms of self-protection until they were above moa-browsing level. It is especially interesting that some plants, such as kowhai, have a divaricating juvenile form on the North and South Islands, but not on off-shore islands where there were no moa.

We can imagine the moa, like feathered, beaked giraffes, wandering along through the forest on tracks as broad as roads. In spite of the defences of some plants, they had plenty to eat and little to fear, and were probably quite placid creatures whose greatest danger was falling into bogs and swamps where they sank like rocks. In fact, most of the moa skeletons which have been found have been preserved in swamps. Perhaps the greatest sub-fossil find was in 1937 in Pyramid Valley, North Canterbury, which was a vast moa grave-yard.

For the millions of years of their existence the moa had few enemies except *Harpagornis*, the giant extinct eagle. Fossils show that it was a forest-dwelling eagle, which killed live prey in preference to eating carrion. It had enormous feet and claws, and powerful wings which enabled it to lift very heavy loads. The moa was amongst its prey.

However it was when man arrived in New Zealand, a thousand years ago, that the moa met its most devastating enemy. The big birds were an obvious source of food in a land without land mammals. The men who arrived here became so expert at hunting them that they have been given the name "moa-hunters". The great birds, twice the size of a man, must have been frightening prey but many means of catching them are described in South Island Maori traditions. Sometimes nets which fell and entangled the birds were hung up in the trees. Often pits were dug on their tracks, covered with sticks and grass to conceal them. Flax nooses were set, which caught the moa by their long necks as they wandered along. Also the birds were pursued by bands of hunters who would drive them into ambushes. Once trapped, they were killed with clubs or spears.

How did the moa react when attacked? They were not completely helpless and witless. They were fast runners with their long legs. As Herries Beattie records: "The moa was a swift bird, and when running against the wind had the habit of keeping its mouth open, hence the proverb, 'a wind-eating Moa'." Their legs were also very powerful, and a rock-drawing by an apprehensive moa-hunter shows a bird, with its leg out as if ready to strike. There were tales that the moa could kill a man or dog with a single kick. Perhaps also they used their long necks and beaks as weapons of self-defence — analyses of the bone structure show that they could probably move their necks in all directions.

During the centuries when man and moa lived together in the land, the moa may have put up a good fight, but it was no match for its human adversary. Huge numbers of moa were killed in various ways, as we know from the large numbers of moa ovens which have been found — rows of them on many different sites. It is estimated that as many as half a million birds were butchered and cooked in the South Island alone. The probable slow rate of reproduction of the moa, combined with constant hunting, meant that eventually they began to die out.

When did the moa become extinct? This is a question which has often been asked, and never answered with certainty. The birds had certainly become extremely rare long before written records. From archaeological and traditional evidence, it seems that they were probably beginning to be an endangered species about 1400 or 1500 A.D. As usual, the birds died out first in the more populated North Island, while they were still a part of life in the South.

However even in the far south, by the nineteenth century when Europeans began exploring the land, the moa had become little more than a distant memory. Yet they were still probably extremely rare rather than extinct. There are stories of fires being lit to clear the land for agriculture, and the odd surviving moa running out from hiding. There were even odd stories of moa being hunted at this time — not perhaps the very largest ones, but still birds taller than a man. Herries Beattie recorded this story at Orepuki:

. . . a solitary Moa turned up after its former mates had left the scene either by way of the Maori oven or by natural death, or by migration to the less frequented regions further back. The bird used to traverse an old Moa track, and while it did no harm to the human beings in the district its very presence was a challenge to the young men. These consulted the old chief as to how they could best accomplish its downfall, and he advised them to dig a pit on the path it usually strolled along. They did so one day, and next morning they found the big bird in the hole and killed it. Some of the participants in this exploit are said to have survived into the whaling era (1830–50).

There were also other stories, from people Herries Beattie considered reliable informants, about the killing of birds which stood about seven feet tall.

Perhaps Europeans even saw the last of the big moa in the nineteenth century — at least they said they did. Two gold prospectors in the "wilds north of Queenstown" reported seeing one in the 1860s:

They were camped under a terrace and had just finished their evening meal and were sitting by the camp fire when a Moa came and stood on the top of the terrace looking down on the camp for a short period. It then turned and leisurely walked away. The two men hastened to the top of the terrace, but as it was getting dark they could not get another sight of their unusual visitor . . .

They describe it as about 8 ft 6 in or 9 ft high, and from the knee downwards its legs were black. The feathers were a lightish grey colour and the head was extremely mobile. The bird went off with immense strides, and where it had been standing they found a pile of its dirt. Quinn stood over 6 ft and was powerfully made; he put his large hand in the footmark but could not span within 3 in of it, measuring from thumb to the middle finger tip. From the depth of the footprints in the soft ground the bird must have been a good weight. Coming to a small flat the men noticed that the hearts of several cabbage trees had been pulled out and partly eaten, and this they considered was done by the Moa. They decided to leave this uncanny region, and in about a week were back in Queenstown. Their story was much doubted, but to his dying day Quinn stoutly maintained its truth. Several times he tried to get Canterbury Maoris to go with him in a quest for the Moa, and it was a Maori who directed my attention to the matter.

In the nineteenth century, stories of the *Dinornis* were likely to be considered tall tales. However it seems quite likely that the smaller varieties of moa may still have been about. In 1880, a little girl, Alice McKenzie, saw a mysterious bird on a remote western coast. As she wrote in her book *Pioneers of Martins Bay*:

Museum reconstruction of Dinornis. Photo Colorview Ltd

Following page *Moa country, Frenchmans Gully, South Canterbury.* Photo Rod Morris

It was in 1880, when I was seven years old, that I first saw the large bird that I now think must have been some kind of moa. I remember it distinctly. It was lying on the sand under the flax which grows on the edge of the bush inside the sand hills on the sea shore.

She found that the bird had no tail, as she parted the feathers of its rounded rump. Then she touched its leg, and the creature turned on her with a "harsh grunting cry" knocking her over and sending her running home. Afterwards her father found very large three-toed footprints in the sand. Many years later, she wondered whether the big bird had been a moa. But when she said it had been a bluish colour, people said it had probably been a takahe. Then Alice McKenzie went to see the mounted takahe in the Otago Museum, and decided it could not possibly have been the bird she saw and touched as a child. For one thing it was too small. Also the takahe had a large beak and stout legs of vivid pink, whereas the bird she remembered had stood up on dark legs.

Alice McKenzie's experience must be taken seriously — and hers is not the only one. As late as the mid-1940s, Jules Berg, a very experienced bushman, was camped at Kisbee Bay at the mouth of Preservation Inlet. In the night he heard splashing close by his tent. He went out to investigate, thinking it may have been a deer, and his torch shone on a group of four very large birds with bodies the size of swans and long necks. They were wading through the water on thick un-swanlike legs. Although he told no one about it for many years, he was convinced that what he had seen was a group of moa.

It seems unlikely that anyone will ever again see a living moa. Yet remarkably we are still finding out more about these extinct birds, and gaining unexpected glimpses of what they may have been like. Only a few years ago, in 1980, an extremely well-preserved skeleton, with some reddish feathers still attached was found in a remote low-rainfall area of Southland. And no one knows what the sub-fossil bones in caves have yet to reveal. The moa ruled this land for perhaps a hundred million years, since before New Zealand left Gondwana. It has left traces which will take a long time to disappear.

Early rock drawing depicting moa. Photo Rod Morris, courtesy Canterbury Museum

Kiwi
The Hidden Bird

WE ALSO FILMED THE FLIGHTLESS kiwi for the BBC co-production "Birds of Paradox". Strangely enough, our task of filming this living bird was almost as difficult as the task of filming the extinct moa.

The kiwi is a bird of the night. One reason the Natural History Unit had never taken its cameras into the bush to make a documentary about kiwis was because of the extreme difficulty of seeing them for more than a few fleeting glimpses.

We knew we had little hope of getting the film we wanted in the dark and difficult conditions of the bush, so our director decided to film the kiwi in the Kiwi House at Otorohanga. This Kiwi House is a tribute to chemist and kiwi enthusiast, Barry Rowe, and other members of the Otorohanga Zoological Society. It enables a steady stream of visitors to see the kiwi under near natural conditions. The air-conditioned "nocturnal house" was built on public domain land after much careful planning by members of the Zoological Society (originally just called the "kiwi club"). A bush floor was laid down to a depth of four feet and landscaped to duplicate the bush. Sprinklers provided intermittent rain. Elaborate cool lighting was installed, so that the birds could experience their normal cycle of day and night — but out of phase with the world outside. The kiwi's "night" coincides with the daylight hours of the human visitors.

Here we hoped to show the birds moving about and feeding. We also wanted to show what goes on in a kiwi burrow. Most of all we wanted to show a kiwi chick actually emerging from its egg.

First, though, our set-building department had to construct polystyrene kiwi burrows with glass walls, so that we could see what went on inside the burrow, and, this took some time.

Even when we were ready to begin filming, our task was far from simple. As with many birds, the kiwis we were working with had strong individual personalities. The female was perky, but the male was sleepy and crafty. Both of them were very sensitive to our lights, even though we had arranged special cool lighting for filming them. They would run away and hide, and refuse to co-operate. The cameraman spent hours with his camera at the ready, without getting any of the shots we wanted.

Finally though he did get some good footage of the kiwi moving about and probing the earth for food with its long bill, showing some of this bird's strange characteristics. The kiwi is the only living bird with nostrils at the end of its bill. Its sense of smell is exceptionally strong for a bird. (Most birds have little or no sense of smell.) As the kiwi has very weak eyesight, it locates the worms it eats by sniffing the earth. Then it taps at

Kiwi habitat. Photo Rod Morris

the worm's burrow, broadens the opening, and draws the worm out. (It can pick and choose amongst many different kinds of worm, as New Zealand has an exceptional variety, with 178 native species and fourteen introduced species.)

After days of waiting, the cameraman also gained some unusual insights into burrow life — especially as he filmed the various positions in which kiwis sleep. Like many birds, the kiwi often turns its head back against its body and tucks its head under its wing — but the kiwi has a twenty centimetre-long beak and a wing the size of a bent matchstick. In this position it looked ridiculous and delightful. At other times the birds were seen lying on their backs with their feet in the air — something which had never been seen before. Such postures are possibly restricted to the safety and privacy of the burrow. Natural history filming can sometimes result in new insights into animal behaviour.

The aspect of kiwi life which we were most anxious to film was the hatching of a kiwi egg, a sight very rarely seen and never before filmed. The kiwi egg is one of the most remarkable features of this most unusual bird. It is about 180 mm long and 80 mm in diameter — six times as large as would be normal for a bird of its weight. One would expect the kiwi to have an egg about the size of a hen's egg. In fact the kiwi's egg is almost exactly the size of remains of bush moa eggs which have been found — which has led to speculations about whether the kiwi was once a very much larger bird. In any case, the carrying of the great egg is a tremendous feat for the female kiwi. Barry Rowe told us that the pregnant female's belly bulges so much with an egg inside it that it touches the ground. It makes up 18% to 25% of her body weight. Females sometimes soak their bellies in puddles of cold water when they are heavy with egg — to relieve the inflamed stretched skin, and to rest the load for a while.

In the wild, when the egg is laid, the female leaves the incubation to the male. This is another big job as the average incubation time is seventy-five days, almost twice the norm for a bird — and about the same time as the gestation period of a mammal of similar size. Once it was thought that the incubation period was so long because the egg was too big for the kiwi to incubate properly. However it now seems more likely that it is because the kiwi has a low body temperature for a bird, about 38°C — similar to the temperature of a mammal.

In the Kiwi House, the male is spared the long task of incubation, as Barry Rowe puts the egg in an incubator. This avoids some of the hazards which might cost the future chick its life, such as the father accidentally breaking the shell with his foot. So it was to the incubator that we went for our film of the egg hatching.

The cameraman trained his camera on to the precious egg, and began a three-day wait, watching day and night the long drawn-out process of the kiwi birth. At first the egg just jiggled around slightly. It would sit for twenty minutes, and then jiggle again. We watched and filmed. Then came the first sign of the chick coming out into the world. A tiny hole appeared in the shell, and the kiwi baby poked the pink tip of its bill through, so that it could get a good supply of air. The egg lay still for about twelve hours while the chick slept after this effort. Then the shell began flexing, belling out, and showing every

Kiwi in nest burrow with egg. Photo Rod Morris

sign that the chick inside was struggling to break out. It was pushing at the shell with its still concealed feet. (Unlike most birds the kiwi has no egg-tooth, but kicks its way out of the shell.) Slowly a crack ran around the shell.

Just at that moment our lights blew! It was a cameraman's nightmare, as we rushed for new bulbs. We got them just in time to film the new-born chick as it slid out of the shell — a very large chick with eyes already open and soft, pink beak and feet. It just lay there on its side, thoroughly exhausted and unable to stand up, because its large belly was attached to a yolk sac which would slowly drain into its body over the next few days, and provide it with food.

Barry Rowe told us that in four to five days, the baby kiwi would be able to move around, and he would move it into the Kiwi House. It would not need to be fed by its parents, but would be able to forage for its own food. In all respects it would be like a miniature adult kiwi — even able to fight and fend for itself if necessary.

Our crew felt privileged to have watched the birth of a kiwi baby — it had seemed more like the birth of a baby mammal than the hatching of a bird chick. It was easier to understand why the American scientist William Calder III had described the bird as "an honorary mammal". In the benevolent environment of early New Zealand, with no mammalian predators, it had evolved more mammalian characteristics than any other bird. The other scenes of kiwi life had been something of a privilege for us too. With the help of the people at Otorohanga we had been able to enter a hidden world.

We also began to understand some of the reasons why the kiwi has not become an endangered species. One reason is the size of the egg — it is too big for small mammalian predators to attack successfully. A second reason is the size and independence of the kiwi chick when it emerges from the egg.

Perhaps however the main reason is that, unlike most of our endangered birds, the kiwi is a very strong fighter. The legs and feet are extremely powerful, making up about a third of the bird's body weight, and the claws are very sharp. Although we had not filmed the kiwis defending themselves, Barry Rowe told us of one of his experiences at the Kiwi House:

One night as I was walking through the pens I disturbed a female kiwi feeding with her chick. She must have felt that her chick was in danger because she kicked him away. I could hear him squeal as he "sailed" through the air and landed in the scrub six metres away. With her chick out of danger she then attacked me, kicking with her strong feet and slashing with her claws. An angry kiwi can be frightening if it attacks you in the dark.

The kiwi has survived in spite of various depredations. The Maori hunted the birds, though sparingly. Only chiefs were allowed to eat kiwi meat and wear soft kiwi cloaks. The Maori believed that the kiwi was under the special protection of the god Tane, and they called it "Te manu a Tane" — "the bird that Tane hid". There were special chants and rituals before a kiwi-hunt — such as this hunt described in 1849, in which the bird was attracted by the prospect of one of its favourite foods, the glow-worm:

Brown kiwi chick. Photo Rod Morris

When it was quite dark they again entered the forest, the tohunga holding a small torch, or rohe, made of the bark of the Kahikatoa (manuka) which was only allowed to glimmer like a glowworm. As they proceeded along the line the tohunga walked first and occasionally imitated the cry of the bird — ho-i-re, ho-i-re — by putting his little finger in his mouth and giving a sharp shrill whistle. The kiwi, supposing it to be the call of its mate, hastened to the spot whence the sound came, and mistaking the light of the torch for the glowworm, rushed upon it, when the man behind lengthened the cord and encouraged the dog to spring upon it, taking special care to keep hold of the leash. . . .

Then came the European threats. As Maori hunters had known, dogs are a predator lethal to kiwis. The bird's chest structure, without protective wing muscles, is very weak. Dogs can kill kiwis just by picking them up in their mouths. European settlers introduced large numbers of dogs to this country, and as with other domestic animals some of them ran wild. There were packs of feral dogs roaming parts of the countryside in the nineteenth century, which killed large numbers of kiwis.

The settlers themselves, often with the help of dogs, also made large-scale attacks on the birds. One man near Nelson, in the 1860s, boasted that "with the aid of two dogs he could catch about fifteen to twenty of them every night. He and his men lived on Kiwi-meat." Kiwis were also killed to be stuffed as museum specimens, and that their skins might be used for feather trimmings and for the muffs which were fashionable in Victorian times.

In fact the kiwi faced many of the dangers the huia faced, yet because of its large eggs and aggressive behaviour, it managed to survive the harsh days of the nineteenth century. In 1896, it became a protected species, and by then the plagues of feral dogs were dying out. The massacre was over — and only one species of kiwi had become rare, the smallest and least aggressive Little Spotted Kiwi (which now survives only on Kapiti Island). To this day the North Island and South Island Brown Kiwi are still quite common in some areas, the Great Spotted Kiwi is still found in North West Nelson, and the Stewart Island Kiwi is still found on the island from which it takes its name. It is a remarkable feat of survival for New Zealand's most ancient bird.

Of course the kiwi still faces dangers which could threaten its existence if we are not careful. In forests possum traps are often set which kill and maim the birds. In areas where they are common they are also run over by cars on remote country roads. Although they are fast runners, like most native ground birds they often freeze in the face of unexpected danger. Perhaps the greatest threat is from the destruction of their habitat, especially large areas of scrubland in Northland.

A few dedicated volunteers from the Otorohanga Zoological Society have been trying to carry out rescue operations in areas where kiwi habitat is being destroyed. This means driving for six hours to Northland on every available weekend, rescuing kiwis from forest which is about to be destroyed, and shifting them to safer forests — a slow and thankless task. A small group of kiwi enthusiasts in the middle of the North Island are amongst the few who are taking responsibility for the survival of our national bird.

A modern kiwi-feather cloak and its maker, Diggeress Te Kanawa. Photo Rod Morris

Following page Little Spotted Kiwi. Brown kiwi. Photo Rod Morris

Kea
Clown of the Mountains

EVERYONE WHO GOES INTO the mountains has their favourite story of keas. Perhaps our most telling experience was when we were trying to film a slow-motion sequence of a kea in flight, to open our *Wild South* programmes. We wanted to show the bird flying directly towards the viewer, its dark-green wings rising and falling to show the spectacular red-and-yellow undersurface. Such slow-motion filming requires extremely bright lights, and the lights we were using were 2000 watts. They generated such heat that the cameraman himself kept well away from them. He began filming, and the kea flew straight towards him as he wanted. Then he realised that the bird was simply heading straight for the most exciting thing it had seen in many a moon — the fiercely blazing lamp. He only just succeeded in deflecting its headlong flight. "What a crazy bird!" he said later. "What other wild bird would deliberately fly into a 2000-watt light?" We'd been afraid beforehand that the bird would be frightened by our activities, but found that the kea just couldn't get enough of the unusual entertainment.

Another cameraman was trying unsuccessfully to find a kea on a mountain slope, when his production assistant saw him coming back with a long line of keas following single-file behind him. A climber, A. P. Harper, described a similar incident:

The Keas, having settled on the ice, began to follow in a long straggling line, about fifteen of them. They have a preternaturally solemn walk, but when in a hurry they hop along on both feet, looking very eager and very much in earnest . . .

The ice was undulating, with little valleys and hummocks. . . .

To judge by their expressions and manners they were in a great state of anxiety on emerging from a hollow to a hummock as to whether I was still there. Now and then the one in front would appear craning his neck, and, on seeing me still ahead, would turn round and shriek "Ke-a," as much as to say "It is all right, boys; come along . . ."

Climbers have many tales of keas, as the birds live in the high mountainous country of the South Island — an area about 850 km long, lofty, precipitous and cold. It seems an unusual home for one of the bright, friendly parrot family, and the kea is the only mountain parrot in the world. (One theory is that the bird had made its home in that region before the mountains began rising, and stayed there as the environment became higher and colder.) Trampers and climbers get to know the kea, with its irrepressible sense of play. Napping trampers, resting from their exertions, may well awake to find keas have untied their boot-laces and stolen them. Keas enjoy going through packs, too, and of course tents are an open invitation. Most climbers realise that the mountain huts

Kea, or mountain parrot. Photo Rod Morris

are their best bet for a good night's sleep — if they are careful to keep the kea out. A piece of doggerel verse was found posted in an alpine hut a few years ago:

I beseech you, dear comrades, to please close the door,
For the kea is coming and they mess on the floor.
There's some that remember, there's some that don't know,
So be a good bunch — close the door when you go.

But even when keas are kept outside the huts, they can be a nuisance. One story tells of how some climbers were bedded down for the night when keas arrived and began playing on the corrugated iron roof. They used the roof as a slide, coasting down, then gleefully shrieking as they flapped back up from the bottom of the roof. When they got bored with this, they brought up stones and rolled them down, sliding after them with more merry shrieks. The tired climbers wanted to sleep, so they thumped on the inside of the iron roof with a broomstick. The noise stopped, and then the climbers inside noticed that a kea was hanging upsidedown outside their window, looking in. The noisy games began again, but now the upsidedown kea was watching for the reaction of the climbers, to find out the cause of the thumping inside the hut. This story is typical of innumerable tales of kea intelligence.

One family got to know the character of the kea better than most of us ever will. Sir Robert Falla, the distinguished ornithologist once brought home a deserted kea chick from a trip into the Southern Alps. His wife, Molly Falla, in her book *A Kea On My Bed* describes her husband opening the box: "Out popped a fluffy little head with bright twinkly brown eyes which were alight with intelligence." Mr Kea, as they called the new member of the family, was a constant source of amusement as they watched him growing up:

What he most wanted to know was how things worked, and he would pull corks from bottles and attempt to put them in again, or prise lids from tins, playing a kind of football with them and rolling them noisily about the room.

Perhaps one story in particular shows the young bird's comic temperament:

One morning, Bob accidentally trod on his foot and Mr Kea's reaction was most vociferous. After being caressed and comforted, however, he apparently quite forgot about the sore foot, much as a child might have done when it has been kissed and 'made better'. That evening he began to run as usual to the door to welcome his master home. Suddenly, a few feet from the door, he pulled up and scowled at Bob and, lifting one foot, came limping back to me. As he had shown no sign whatever of limping during the day, the family's mirth was prodigious — it became more so when we realised he was holding up the wrong foot!

The intelligence and curiosity of the kea have not always been regarded with such affection. In fact the kea, at one time, was the most persecuted bird in New Zealand. Many of our birds have been destroyed accidentally, when new predators were introduced to this land, or humans killed too many of them. The intelligent, amusing kea is

Kea stealing pipe. Photo Rod Morris

the only bird we have ever deliberately set out to exterminate — so his is a story worth telling.

It began when farmers came into the high country in the nineteenth century. Keas had probably seldom seen people before. (The Maori regarded mountains as being tapu, and tended to keep away from them.) Certainly kea had never seen sheep. But when they found the skin and entrails of dead sheep hung up on fences, they quickly learned to peck at them — especially in winter, when their usual food of grubs and berries was hard to get. Then it didn't take long for the kea to learn to peck at live sheep, for the same fatty food. The wound the kea left often became poisoned so that the sheep died.

The first person to describe a kea attacking a sheep in this way is believed to be James McDonald, head shepherd at Lake Wanaka Station:

I do not know whether I was the first to see the Kea attack sheep, but I was the first to report it to Mr Henry Campbell of Wanaka Station. . . . In 1868 my orders were to go all over the run after the snowfall and see that the sheep were evenly distributed over the ground, that no hill or spur had more sheep on it than it could well carry. While I was at this work, the snow being about 2 ft deep, I went out to the tops; in a small basin . . . there was a mob of sheep snowed in and unable to get out. There I saw the Kea at work. He would come down from the rocks, settle on the sheep's loin, and peck into the sheep, which would run through the mob; but the bird stuck to the sheep all the time till he got a piece out of it; then he would fly to the rocks. I watched the bird at this work and did not disturb him until I was fully satisfied. . . .

Then I went down to the station and reported to Mr Campbell. He would not credit me, and all hands at the station refused to believe that the birds would do it. . . .

The men at Lake Wanaka Station believed the story when they were taken to see for themselves, and soon it was becoming only too well-known that some kea attacked sheep. Usually it was in winter, when the birds were hungry. The sheep were often easy prey in the snow. When their usual foods were plentiful, the kea usually left the sheep alone. Even in hungry times, not all kea attacked sheep. One musterer described the signs: "You can always tell a killer-kea, he's got socks on him. Wool, round his legs, where he's been hanging on to the sheep."

However most sheep farmers were not concerned to make distinctions. They were just angry that any of their sheep were dying. Of course the kea were not the greatest hazard they had to face in the cliff-ridden, snow-bound high country they had decided to farm, but there was not much they could do about the topography or the weather, whereas there was a great deal they could do about keas. It wasn't long before war was being declared.

The government was asked to help, and obliged the pastoralists by authorising local Councils to pay a bounty for the destruction of keas. The amount seems to have ranged from 2s 6d to £1 for kea beaks. Kea hunting became a way of life. Shepherds and musterers carried firearms so that they could kill any kea they saw. Also a new breed of bounty hunters sprang up who could earn more money at killing keas than they could at any other available job. It was a rugged life, which often meant going into precipitous

Victims of the kea hunter. Photo Rod Morris, courtesy Canterbury Museum

country, but it paid off handsomely. Strings of kea heads flooded into County Council Offices. One kea hunter (about 1870) was paid a lump sum of £500, and during the same year thousands of pounds were paid to other hunters in the Wanaka district alone.

As the campaign to wipe out the kea progressed, the stories of kea atrocities grew in number and ferocity. All keas were described as cruel, murderous carnivores who loved to torture their innocent victims, and often rode their backs maniacally until the sheep were driven over cliffs to their deaths. One account described the sheep as being "dashed to pieces" on the rocks below. The keas were then said to descend on the hapless forms to tear them to bits and devour them. Even Sir Walter Buller wrote in his *History of New Zealand Birds:* "In some parts of the country the Kea menace has risen to such a pitch that the run-holders have been driven off the country." He quoted a newspaper report which said: "Mr D. A. Cameron, one of our oldest run-holders in the Lake County, Otago, is throwing up his run in the Nokomai, through the Keas, which, if not more numerous, are according to reports becomer greater adepts at the destruction of sheep." Buller thought that the birds would soon be exterminated.

However, by the early twentieth century, some people were beginning to have doubts about the war between keas and sheep. In 1907, when he was writing a book called *The Kea: A New Zealand Problem,* G. R. Marriner thought he should look into some of the worst stories, and wrote to Mr D. A. Cameron whom Buller had described as being driven from his run by keas. He received the following reply:

Dear Sir,

My son Alec has handed me your letter of the 19th inst., re "Kea". There is no truth in the statement that I ever intended to give up my run owing to excessive damage done by Keas. Many years ago we had a few here, but they did not do much damage to sheep. . . . I have no idea where Mr Buller and the papers got their information.

Yours truly,
(signed) D. A. Cameron

By this time, after the years of massacre, kea were becoming much more scarce, and Marriner also wrote that many men on sheep runs did not bother to carry guns now, as there was so little chance of shooting a kea.

During the twentieth century, gradually more moderate attitudes began to prevail. At last, in 1970, a law was passed to protect kea fully in national and forest parks and reserves. Elsewhere the birds were protected from sportsmen, but not from sheep farmers if they claimed to be acting in protection of their flocks.

Then, in 1986, newspapers carried the report, *"Kea to Become Fully Protected":*

The Minister of Internal Affairs, the Hon. P. Tapsell, said last night that he hoped to pass protecting legislation this year to prevent the extinction of the birds, which may now number as low as 1000.

"Now is the time to rescue uncommon and declining birds, rather than waiting until they reach the brink of extinction," he said.

Probably the number of keas left is not as low as 1000 — perhaps more like 5000. Still there are certainly far fewer than there once were. Official figures show that over 150,000

Kea chicks. Photo Lionel Lobb

Following page A kea reveals the bright red feathers of underwing and rump. Photo Rod Morris

birds have been killed over the past century. Philip Temple, whose novel, *Beak of the Moon*, attempts to give a kea's eye view of the world, calls this deliberate slaughter "the worst case of avicide in New Zealand's history."

We must feel glad that, for the moment, the kea has been saved to amuse us, surprise us, even annoy us and damage our property, and cheekily remind us that this ancient land was not made just for the benefit of the human race.

How long will our new-found human tolerance last? We now have a burgeoning tourist industry, and the mountains of the South Island are one of the big attractions.

Keas love places where people congregate, such as ski resorts. Often they join in the winter sports, and are seen following people around with their bouncing, dancing hop. They slide happily down the iron roofs, and walk behind each other up the tow-lift cables. They also toboggan down the ski-slopes, slowing themselves by toeing their feet in a V-formation as the skiers do. There are many fine ski-fields in the world, but only those in New Zealand have the added attraction of performing keas. But as always New Zealanders have a love-hate relationship with the kea, and not all of the birds' antics at the ski-fields are popular.

Their love of mischief can range from nuisance to minor destruction. They prise snug-fitting lids off rubbish tins with their powerful beaks, and scatter the rubbish about. A kea-proof rubbish tin has yet to be invented. In car parks they can cause serious damage if their games include cracking plastic tail-lights, chewing windscreen-wiper blades, or pulling out soft rubber seals around the windows. Motorists leaving tyre-valve caps off have returned to discover that the kea, quite clever with the operation of valves, has let air out of their tyres. Keas have been known to turn on taps and take fuses from fuseboxes. The kea plays with everything. When a few keas ripped some chair-lift seat-covers, stripped electrical wiring, and also had their way in an unclosed van, the operator of one ski-field persuaded the Wildlife Service to remove half a dozen delinquent keas from his resort. To his surprise, the public outcry was such that the keas have now been returned. The clown of the mountains seems to be winning a steadily increasing audience.

Not everyone though shares the feelings of the kea's friends. A letter to an Otago newspaper in 1986 put the other side of the case:

Sir, — Shooting keas is something I have been in favour of for a long time . . . The kea is a nice-looking bird, and nobody likes to see the bird now and again more than I do, but we have to remember that the tourist industry is the only hope we have got. If these keas are attacking tourists and their equipment up in the mountains, then they will have to go, and that is that. It is not a matter of the odd sheep here and there, it is the future of the country. New Zealand needs the tourist dollar, and if the birds get in the way, tough luck for them. . . .

Of course this comment shows misunderstanding of what many tourists want to see — the famous mountain parrot is more an asset than a liability to the tourist industry. But it also shows the kea's remarkable capacity for getting under our skins. It seems that the bird will always be the subject of much heated debate.

Kea country, Tutoko. Photo Rod Morris

Chapter Three

Takahe

The Lost and Found Bird

BY THE EARLY TWENTIETH CENTURY, the takahe, or *Notornis,* was believed to be extinct. Its stuffed and mounted remains stood in the British Museum, not far from the remains of a dodo, both birds attracting thousands of visitors daily. The takahe was a large and brightly-coloured bird, with a beautiful range of deep blues and greens in its plumage, a big scarlet beak and waxy-pink legs.

Very few takahe had ever been seen by European eyes, although long ago the Maori had probably dined frequently on the large meaty bird. The first written record of its existence came after Walter Mantell unearthed its bones in the moa-beds at Waingongoro in the North Island. While the Maori had known it as "takahe" or "moho", in 1847 it was christened *Notornis mantelli,* in honour of its recent discoverer.

Two years later Walter Mantell discovered another takahe in the South Island — but with one exciting difference. The bird he found here was alive! That was in 1849, and the account proudly read by his illustrious father Dr Gideon Mantell to the Zoological Society in London on the 12th of November, 1850, is a graphic document:

This bird was taken by some sealers who were pursuing their avocations in Dusky Bay. Perceiving the trail of a large and unknown bird on the snow with which the ground was covered, they followed the footprints till they obtained a sight of the Notornis, *which their dogs instantly pursued, and after a long chase caught alive in the gully of a sound behind Resolution Island. It ran with great speed, and upon being captured uttered loud screams, and fought and struggled violently; it was kept alive three or four days on board the schooner and then killed, and the body roasted and ate by the crew,each partaking of the dainty, which was declared to be delicious.*

It was Mantell's good fortune to come upon the scene of preparations for the cooking. He obtained the complete skin, which became the first takahe to be mounted and displayed in the British Museum.

Two years later, in 1851, Mantell obtained another takahe skin, this time from a Maori on Secretary Island in Thompson Sound. This soon joined the first one in the British Museum, where they were presumed to be male and female.

Twenty-eight years were to elapse until, in 1879, a third specimen was taken, on the eastern side of Lake Te Anau. A rabbiter's dog caught the bird and the rabbiter took it from him alive, but killed it and hung it on the ridge pole of his tent. The station

Scientist Jim Mills studying takahe tracks in the snow. Photo Rod Morris

manager, a Mr J. O'Connor, was doing his rounds and noticed it. The rabbiter gave it to him and he took it back to the station, skinning it and carefully preserving all the bones. He shipped this material on the *Waitangi* to England for sale and it went up for auction at Stevens Rooms in Covent Garden where it was bought by the Dresden Museum for £105. It remained on display there until it was destroyed by the bombs which devastated that city during World War II.

It was almost twenty years before the fourth *Notornis* was captured. In 1898 Jack and Donald Ross, camping on the shores of the Middle Fiord, heard an unusual bird call. Their dog 'Rough' ran into the bush and came back with a bird in his mouth. The brothers took it to the Otago Museum where the Curator, Sir William Benham, became the first man to dissect a takahe. He found it to be a healthy young female with its stomach full of swamp plants, confirming Maori belief about its vegetarian nature. The New Zealand Government purchased this one for £250 and it was stuffed and mounted for the Otago Museum, where it is still on display. Later the remains of a fifth takahe were found on the east side of Lake Te Anau, but only in the form of a skeleton. For fifty years the Otago Museum's takahe was regarded as the best specimen of its kind, and the last one which had been found alive.

It was this specimen, sitting glass-eyed in the museum in Dunedin which provided the inspiration for the eventual startling re-discovery of the living *Notornis*.

In 1919 the *Otago Witness* included a poster featuring a photograph of the stuffed takahe and the sheet was kept by a Mrs Orbell of Oamaru. Her son Geoffrey recalls his fascination with this poster when he was about eleven years old:

I can remember asking my mother about this bird, and she always said it was supposed to be extinct. And I can still remember asking her what 'extinct' meant, and she said, "Well it's supposed to be dead." It was always 'supposed to be'. I must have asked other questions, but I always had that phrase in the back of my mind. Then of course when I was at Varsity I was able to follow that up by seeing the actual takahe in the museum in Dunedin.

Geoffrey Orbell graduated from Otago Medical School to become a specialist practitioner in Invercargill, on the highroad to Fiordland. His love of hunting, fishing and tramping in wild country took him out into the mountains on all possible weekends and holiday spells, with a few close friends. By his own account he never lost that curiosity about the possible survival of takahe:

On one hunting trip I met a forest warden named Norman Murrell. He had spent his childhood beside Lake Manapouri, on the fringe of the Notornis *area. He told me stories of calls he had heard in the bush and of blurred tracks he had seen on sandy beaches.*

In 1929 I went deerstalking up the north arm of Lake Te Anau. I kept a sharp lookout for all bird tracks, but only found those of weka or kiwi. On this trip I met a ranger whose name was Charles Evans. He told me about tracks he had seen in Dusky Sound — of a whole boat's crew dashing here and there on the beach trying to catch a bird the size of a goose, with blue-green feathers and the speed of a racehorse. And he told me also about tracks up in the snowgrass.

From rumours and stories told around campfires at night, while stags roared challenges across high valleys, I picked up little bits of information. Another ranger, Ward Beer, told me of a large blue bird seen on the shores of Lake Ada, which he thought might be a pukeko. And a patient of mine who once lived at Martins Bay told me of a large blue bird seen there.

In 1945 he built a holiday house at Te Anau and he and his friends decided to make a systematic probe of some of the long valleys, known as "burns", extending into the Murchisons. Nobody had really looked at this area before, apart from a brief search of the lower Ettrick Burn for wapiti in 1932. So Dr Orbell's group became the first Europeans ever really to explore the Murchison mountains — and this was as late as the end of World War II!

The deep and rough-cut burns fanned out from the peaks and made their way down to Lake Te Anau. Their steep contours, covered with dense bush, made progress slow and difficult. Still Dr Orbell's party began at the north end of the Murchisons with the Snag Burn, moved round to the Ettrick Burn — the longest of the valleys, and over the next two years worked around the whole circuit of valleys. In all this time they saw no tracks or signs of takahe, except for some suspicious droppings high in the Ettrick Burn. However Dr Orbell had not lost the obsession, carried with him from childhood, that the great blue-green bird with the heavy scarlet beak and legs, was only "supposed" to be extinct. He remembers:

On wet days and long evenings in Te Anau I would study the map of Fiordland I had pinned on the wall. Each time I looked at that map I became more interested. Was the Notornis *still about? It was a question I often asked myself. I seldom spoke about it to others, except to mention it or joke about it to odd people whom I thought might have stories of their own to tell.*

One man who knew Fiordland well volunteered the information that in a certain area (he wouldn't say where) he always carried a special bullet in his rifle. The bullet might be worth four or five hundred pounds, he said. He would have shot any Notornis *he saw, for the money. But that was just another link in the chain. Studying the map and thinking about the stories, I began to realise they were all similar in one respect; all the birds were seen or caught on beaches below the bushline. And as far as I could make out from books and from other reports all these birds were seen or taken in years of very heavy snowfall. By plotting all references on my map it became apparent that there was a vast area of unexplored Fiordland surrounded by reported instances of* Notornis *being found or seen.*

I heard stories of a large lake seen from the air. Maori history told of a lake Te Wai-o-pani — *'The Lake of the Friendless' — located on the western side of Lake Te Anau, above some cliffs. It was reputed to be where the lost tribe had once lived.*

Dr Orbell developed a strengthening hunch that they had to get above the valleys and search the high tops. At last he and his small party decided to act on the idea. They went back into the Ettrick Burn, but instead of proceeding into the valley they turned left and began an arduous ascent up the bush-covered mountain-side toward the high plateaux and shallow hanging valleys which form hammocks in the roof of the Murchison Mountains. His own recollection of that day best conveys the drama of it.

We first went into that country on April 11, 1948. There were three of us — Rex Watson, Neil McCrostie and myself. It was very tough going and took over four hours climbing to get to the top. We came onto the ridge suddenly and looked over — to find ourselves on the edge of a terrific precipice. Far below us a large lake glistened in the sun, and a valley filled with snowgrass extended three miles beyond it. The cliffs were so high that I could only just make out a young stag in the valley almost directly below us.

We scrambled around great overhanging bluffs and eventually managed to find a route by which we slid and scrambled down to the valley floor. Here we boiled a billy of water for a brew, and then separated to shoot roaring stags. I shot a poor 14-pointer and sat down about halfway up the valley to wait for the others.

While I was dozing in the snowgrass I heard a bird call which I didn't recognise — two long deep notes repeated twice. I was very tired and I just sat and wondered about them. When Rex and Neil returned they both accused me of whistling to them by blowing across the top of an empty ·303 cartridge case. It was then mid-afternoon, a little late to go off investigating noises and run the risk of being caught out in the bush overnight. Rather than attempt the awful climb out of the valley, we decided to push on and try to get out by way of the gorge below the lake.

On a beach at the bottom end of the lake we found fresh bird tracks. They were large enough for us to be quite certain that they were the tracks I had dreamed about. The sun was already sinking behind the mountains and we had to hurry to get down through 2000 feet of bush before dark, so I measured the tracks as carefully as possible by scratching marks on the stem of my pipe — which is practically always in my mouth and therefore less likely to get lost.

One might wonder how Dr Orbell could feel so certain that 'these were the tracks' of a bird he had never seen alive and which was regarded as extinct for half a century. But Orbell had developed his observational skills very early in life:

Even when I first looked at the mounted takahe in the Otago Museum, when I was a University medical student, I noticed the back kick on the toe. I knew the tracks of the pukeko, I knew the tracks of gulls — and of course the tracks of a wading bird are totally different from the tracks of a swimming bird because you've always got the curved toes on a swimming bird and you've got the straight toes on a wading bird. But there's no bird that had the toe going off to one side. When I first saw those tracks I knew this was it. I just said, "There you are, boys. We've found him!"

But the experts weren't as confident of the find as was Dr Orbell, when he passed his evidence on to them. He recalls their apparently unconvinced reception of the evidence:

When we got back to Invercargill I put the measurements and a diagram down on paper and sent them to Professor Marples at Otago University. I also compared my measurements with all the published measurements I could find, and they matched these fairly closely. However, Professor Marples replied that he felt that the tracks were too big to be a Notornis *and that he thought they were probably those of a White Heron. Dr Robert Falla of the National Museum in Wellington was the next to see my diagrams, but he did not recognise them as belonging to any bird he knew.*

This professional verdict could have been discouraging, but Dr Orbell merely scoffed at it:

Takahe. Photo Rod Morris

I knew what they were. I wanted some corroboration, but there was nothing else they could be. We all, those who had been in there with me, said "White Heron — ha!" so I said, "Alright, let's make certain that there's nothing else they could be." But we couldn't get back before the snow came down — we had a particularly bad winter that year. We agreed to go back as soon as the spring came round, but one thing led to another and we weren't in any hurry to go back in. Then Neil McCrostie rang me one morning and said, "Hey Doc, have you seen the paper this morning?" I said, "No, what about it?" He said, "Well I see that Marples is going in to explore the country above the Tunnel Burn at Christmas time." So I said, "Alright, we'll go in next week-end. How about it?"

Dr Orbell was soon to recall that momentous week-end in a more sedate style for the London press:

On November 20 we once more made the arduous climb back to the valley.

We returned to where we had found the tracks on our last trip. Suddenly, quite near this spot, a large blue-green bird stepped out from amongst the snow tussock. And there, no more than twenty metres away from us, stood a living Notornis, *the bird that was 'supposed' to be extinct! My first reaction was to think how small it was. It didn't stand much higher than a pukeko. However it was heavier and more sturdily built than a pukeko, with shorter stronger legs.*

We hid ourselves in the snowgrass in case it ran off, and I took a reel of colour movie film. And then another Notornis *arrived, so I took another half reel of film. When I stood up, both birds were no more afraid than farmyard hens, and only moved a metre or so into the snowgrass. The fishing net was quietly circled round them and they simply walked into it and were captured. Everything had gone according to plan.*

Handling them as gently as possible, we took them to the beach where they were securely tethered by one leg, photographed, and then let go again. We didn't wish to disturb them too much because we were certain they had a nest somewhere nearby and we wished the female to return to her eggs as quickly as possible. The nest, I decided, would have to wait for another year, rather than risk driving them away from the nest completely.

The long search was over. The Notornis *wasn't extinct. It just hadn't been 'seen' for over 50 years — simply because no one had known just where to look for them.*

Dr Orbell's news, on that 20th of November 1948, rapidly became world news. A headline in the *Illustrated London News* read *"A Sight Never Before Seen By White Men: The Discovery of a Colony of the 'Extinct'* Notornis, *or Takahe"*. The doctor from Invercargill had become famous overnight. The hidden secret valley of Maori legend which he had looked down on from that high precipice was christened 'Takahe Valley', and the Maori 'Lake of the Friendless' now appears on our maps as 'Lake Orbell'. It had suddenly acquired too many friends, so that steps were required to protect the takahe's mountain retreat from all except those scientifically responsible.

In recognition of his remarkable discovery, Dr Geoffrey Orbell was given an "illuminated address" which was also a special permit making him the only man able to go into that restricted area any time he chose.

Two months after the announcement of the discovery, the first scientific expedition

Drs Falla and Orbell (right) with takahe chick, 1949. Photo J. M. Sorenson, courtesy N.Z. Wildlife Service

Following page *Takahe country, Murchison Mountains.* Photo Rod Morris

was led into Takahe Valley by Dr Orbell, and from that time on scientists went on quietly studying the bird for many years — until in the 1970s, the *Notornis* was in the news again. The Wildlife officers with responsibility for the bird noticed that there seemed to be a sudden fall in its population.

In 1972 a scientist Dr J. A. Mills was given the job of finding out what was happening to the takahe. He organised a count of the birds, and found that, in all the Murchisons, there seemed to be only about 250 takahe left, whereas when they were first rediscovered, there were estimated to be some hundreds. Jim Mills began trying all possible methods of saving the bird.

It was just at this stage that the Natural History Unit of Television New Zealand was set up. The new takahe study proved an ideal subject for our first story. We filmed the work Jim Mills was doing with the takahe — and also interviewed Dr Orbell about the drama of the bird's rediscovery, which had given it such a special place in New Zealand's wildlife. And of course we watched and filmed the private life of the takahe.

The first takahe filming trip has already been described at the beginning of this book — it was a disaster. For our second trip, on the advice of Jim Mills and Roger Lavers (another scientist) we took our filming and sound recording gear into Plateau Creek, a high valley in the heart of the Murchisons at the head of the Ettrick Burn. The scientists said a pair of takahe here were unusually trusting and undisturbed by humans. They had often seen people, but had never been banded or given any reason to feel afraid.

When Jim Mills pointed out the size of their territory, it was huge — a whole hillside rather than a normally-sized bird territory. It seemed an enormous area in which to try to locate a pair of birds. However the scientists had developed a means of attracting the birds by broadcasting a tape-recording of their calls. Takahe make a variety of calls — a hennish cluck when feeding, the occasional frightened screech, a rhythmical *kau-kau* when recalling their chicks, and a percussive note of alarm which the Maori described picturesquely as sounding like the knocking together of pieces of greenstone underwater. The contact call which Jim began broadcasting on his tape-recorder was a low round sound — a sort of *klow-eeep*. This was the call the pair of birds kept making to each other as they moved around, looking for food. When the call was broadcast, we heard a distant response coming back through the still mountain air. After taking repeated bearings on the replies, we could tell that we were coming close to the birds. Then we saw them.

Against the snow, the colours looked brilliant, the blue and green feathers, scarlet beak and bright pink legs. The birds seemed like giant tropical parrots, and strangely out of place in that vast, bleak environment. They moved cautiously over the thin crust of snow with their long splayed toes. One suddenly disappeared and had obviously fallen through the snow into the scrub beneath. A few seconds later it re-appeared with a crown of snow on its head, and continued moving about in a calm and regal way. They were stately-looking birds.

As Jim had expected, they didn't seem at all worried by the presence of our film crew as long as we moved slowly and didn't do anything to alarm them. Our cameraman was soon lying in the tussock and worming his way round amongst them, to get the best close shots. It was exciting to be so near to the birds, when their aura of near-extinction together with the problems of getting to them had made them so remote and inaccessible.

The birds kept on eating steadily. Like many browsing creatures, they have to eat nearly all the time to get enough nourishment — and these browsers have even more work than most. To get each mouthful of food, the takahe has to climb into a tussock, and hold part of it down with its foot, while pulling out a stalk, or tiller, with its massive beak. It picks the tiller up, using its foot like a hand, and eats about three centimetres off the end — the part where the sugar and protein are concentrated. The rest of the stalk is thrown away. Then the bird goes through the whole process again for its next bite of food.

The tussock was as tall as the bird, so it was hard to get close enough to film this clearly. However later, in another area, we got some fine footage of a takahe down in the bush, digging up another of its foods — the root of a fern. The takahe dug the twenty-centimetre root out of the ground, peeled off the hard outer skin, and ate the white starchy part left, clipping this off in short segments. It was fortunate to get film of this, because Jim said that the takahe does not like fern root as much as tussock and eats it only in winter — perhaps because it's not such nutritious food. The bird will walk along frozen stream beds to get the last bits of tussock until it's all completely covered in snow. Only then does it look for fern root in the bush.

Jim and Roger had been doing intensive research into the kinds of foods the takahe ate, as they believed this was a major cause of their decline. At first Jim had thought stoats would be the major problem. Stoats are widespread even through the wildest areas of the Murchisons, and ever since the first scientific expeditions of 1949 it had been known that stoats kill takahe eggs and chicks. Stoat trapping had been intensified in recent years. However most of the takahe pairs Jim studied managed to hatch out their chicks without being attacked by predators. The chicks lived for a few weeks, then just died for no apparent reason.

It seemed that the cause might be poor diet. Amongst all the plants in the Murchisons there are only about five the takahe will eat regularly — three species of tussock, the fern root, and one kind of mountain daisy. Of these, their preferred foods are the protein-and-mineral-rich tussocks. Jim had analysed the tussock in areas where there were most chick deaths, and found that the plants there had less nitrogen, phosphorus and calcium than in areas where takahe were doing well. The previous year he had arranged for some areas to be top-dressed with a fertiliser which should improve the quality of takahe pastures. Now, as he tested the tussocks the takahe ate, he was finding that the birds were consistently selecting plants which had been top-dressed, and rejecting the others. Perhaps he was on the right track.

An obvious underlying reason for the deterioration in tussock quality was the sudden influx of red deer to the Murchisons in the 1950s and 1960s. According to Dr Orbell:

When I first went in there — back when we found the takahe — the bush came right down to the lake. You couldn't have seen more than ten metres along the side of the lake. Now you could shoot a deer fifty metres back — in the open. It's not that they're competing for the same food, but the deer are destroying the actual food patches that the bird has to live on in the winter.

Hunters were shooting up to seventy-five deer in one day, and told of animals swimming across the stretches of water between the arms of the lake.

Deer eat many of the same foods as takahe, and in eating the tussocks on which the takahe are most dependent, they have a disastrous long-term effect on the plants. Whereas takahe pull the tussock tillers out from the base, helping the plant to regenerate, the deer eat the tops of the tillers, leaving the plant damaged and unhealthy. Heavy deer browsing will eventually kill tussocks.

Ultimately Jim Mills and others felt that the only way to improve the takahe's environment was to get rid of the red deer. The Wildlife Service had employed deer cullers for years. Then, in the early 1970s, there was suddenly a commercial demand for deer velvet and helicopter hunting was introduced. Some people were reluctant to allow the helicopter companies into national parks — but Jim Mills was influential in persuading the authorities to allow commercial deer cullers to work in the Murchisons. The numbers of deer were dramatically reduced.

Jim hoped that eventually this might lead to naturally-regenerated takahe pastures. In the meantime, he was hoping that the top-dressing would help see the takahe through their immediate problems.

He said that the particular pair of birds we were filming had been studied for seven years. Each year they had nested and hatched a chick; but each year the chick died. As Jim believed this might have been caused by the poor diet of the mother, he was hoping that in the coming season, after eating the top-dressed tussock, the birds might manage to raise a chick through to independence.

Later that year, at nesting time, our film crew went back to see what happened, and were taken to the takahe nest. It was well-hidden amongst clumps of tussock, which bent over it, sheltering it from the weather and other dangers.

Now that the snow had gone, it was surprising to see how well-camouflaged the takahe were. The blues and greens of their backs merged in with the sage-green tussock so that they were almost invisible. They also seemed to know that their scarlet beaks were a danger — if anything happened to alarm one of the birds, it would hide its head in the nest or a tussock.

We set up our hide, taking care not to disturb the birds. Then we watched and filmed what went on. There were two large eggs in the nest, dull-cream in colour, with brown spots and faint mauve blotches. The parent birds took turns at sitting on the eggs. At changeover time, they moved quickly and quietly, not calling to each other, apparently aware of the dangers of predators.

After the cameraman had been sitting in his hide for many hours, a predator did come. It was not a stoat — the only stoats we saw were caught in traps. It was another native

Takahe pair. Photo Rod Morris

bird, the quick and sometimes destructive weka. The strong-beaked brown bird did not come straight in on the nest, but sized up the situation and went away. The cameraman did not intervene to protect the nest, but decided that the takahe was probably able to defend itself against the smaller native rail. He stayed with his camera, and waited for the weka to return. The weka came back, made a fuss, and left. However when it came back a third time, the cameraman had the satisfaction of seeing the aggressive weka being driven off by the stout and powerful takahe. The weka did not return again that day.

Then at last came the main scene we were waiting for — the hatching of the chick. We saw the mother feeling a movement underneath her, lifting her body away from the eggs, and the little egg-tooth of the first chick pipping through the shell.

Very soon after they were hatched, the two black fluffy chicks began to move around outside the nest. After a day or two, they were going right out into the tussock pastures with their parents. They did not feed themselves though, but stood around making wheedling calls, and waiting for their parents to bring them food.

They were very helpless. For the first month, they would be fed a special diet of insects which their parents scraped out of the earth. Later the adult takahe would still feed their chicks on tussock for weeks before they could get their own food. The parent birds had to work all day and late into the night to get enough food for themselves and their chicks.

The chicks stayed fairly close to their parents while we were there — except when they were alarmed by birds flying overhead. Then they quickly buried themselves in tussock bushes — climbing right in until they were completely hidden. Even when an observer knew there was a chick inside a clump of tussock it was almost impossible to see it. As with many native birds, "freezing" was one of their main means of defence. This worked when their main enemies were birds of prey so sharp-sighted that they could see the slightest movement. Unfortunately it was useless against mammalian predators with their sharp sense of smell.

Again we saw no signs of stoats, although Roger Lavers told of a time when he had come across one of these powerful predators apparently attacking a takahe chick. Roger didn't see what was going on, but heard calling and sounds of violent movement. Then the takahe pair went off with their chick, and Roger came up to find a freshly-killed, decapitated stoat. Adult takahe are large and powerful creatures, and the chicks are probably fairly safe if they don't wander too far away from their parents.

We were delighted that, even at this stage in their lives, when most birds are suspicious of intruders, neither parents or chicks seemed to regard our film crew as a threat, but let us move around quietly amongst them. It seemed miraculous that the parents were prepared to come out with a chick, and feed it, in front of the camera. We felt tremendously privileged to be witnessing these intimate scenes of family life — especially when we remembered all the apprehensions when the Natural History Unit was set up that our work might be a series of literal wild goose chases. Because Jim and Roger had introduced us to such a trusting pair of takahe, we had succeeded in getting better footage than could have been imagined.

It was with these scenes of takahe family life that we planned to finish our first *Wild South* documentary. We wanted to say that another two takahe had been added to the population of the Murchisons. But it didn't turn out that way. While our programme was being edited the two chicks died — like 70% of all takahe chicks. Instead our film closed with scenes of the takahe pastures being top-dressed, and the hope that this improvement of the tussocks might provide the breakthrough for the future of the takahe population.

In fact this didn't happen either. We kept in touch with Jim and Roger over the years following "Project Takahe", to see how the birds were progressing. The pair we had filmed did succeed in raising several chicks to independence, but elsewhere the picture was not so good. In some top-dressed areas, there was even an increase in the number of infertile eggs laid. Possibly this drop in fertility was related to the increasing age of the parent birds in those areas, but it was also possible that the fertiliser was having negative side-effects. Clearly the problem was not as simple as had been hoped.

Over the years, many ways of helping the takahe have been tried: top-dressing, stoat-trapping, deer-culling. There are now far fewer deer in the Murchisons than there have been for a long time. Possibly in the end, the tussock pastures will regenerate naturally, so that the takahe can raise healthy chicks there again; though possibly, too, the small number of deer left will be just enough to stop this happening.

The takahe's problems seem to be more complex than those of any other native bird. Of course, we cannot know how long these problems have been going on. Sub-fossil bones in caves, sand dunes, and swamps show that takahe once lived in lower altitudes throughout New Zealand, where the environment offered a wider variety of foods and was less harsh climatically. Perhaps the takahe were forced up into the mountains because of changes in their former habitats, or predation by man — the stout birds were an important source of food for the pre European Maori. The existing population seems extremely well-adapted as an alpine species, but no one yet understands enough about the historical ecology of the takahe to know what areas it might be able to adapt to in the future — although people are trying to find out.

In the meantime, the best hope is to try to increase the numbers of takahe, so that there is a younger and healthier population base. Recently new strategies have been developed to increase the breeding success of the takahe (techniques which have already been tried with other bird species in New Zealand). In 1983 the Wildlife Service began redistributing eggs from takahe nests, to ensure that each pair was incubating a fertile egg. It had been found over the years that takahe generally only ever managed to raise one chick through to independence. Yet some pairs were wasting their time sitting on infertile clutches of eggs, or even on empty nests. By redistributing the fertile eggs, it has been possible to achieve a doubling of the chick population.

There was a major expansion of this programme in 1985, with the opening of a $200,000 chick-rearing unit, managed by the Wildlife Service in Te Anau. Here any surplus eggs are hatched in special sealed rooms, concealed by one-way glass, so that although the chicks are being watched, they have no contact with any humans. The

Following page *Takahe feeding.* Photo Rod Morris

brooders under which the chicks hatch are shaped like parent takahe. They are wired to maintain the right temperature and to produce the special takahe brooding calls. After seven weeks, when the chicks are old enough to go out on their own, they are taken to a nearby 3000-hectare area of red tussock and beech forest, without having had any direct contact with people. By preventing any possible imprinting from humans during chick raising, it is hoped that the young will adapt quickly to life in their natural environment. Through these techniques, the number of takahe are at last beginning to increase, slightly.

One thing we can be certain about is that the takahe will never disappear because of apathy. It is our most studied and publicised rare bird. It seems almost a miracle to be given back such a large and spectacular bird, believed for so long to be extinct. Most people seem determined now not to let it go.

Takahe nest with eggs. Photo Rod Morris

Previous page *Takahe preening at night time roost.* Photo Rod Morris

Chapter Four

Black Stilt

The Lone Wader

IN NATURAL HISTORY DOCUMENTARIES, as in old newsreels, particular camera shots have a way of stopping time. One such moment was a scene filmed one clear winter's evening, in the high Mackenzie Country, at the foot of the Southern Alps.

The van seemed to have been bumping for hours over rough farm roads. The treeless snow-covered landscape was an awesome sight, with brilliant white mountains floating on the long horizon. It was bitterly cold, and we swapped stories we'd been told of the harsh conditions we would find up here in the heart of winter, and of the hardships faced by livestock and wildlife. There was the tale of a day when thick ice covered the ground — ice so clear that the sheep were found staring through it, at the grass locked beneath. There were terrible stories of the winter of 1895, when Balmoral and Glenmore Stations lost 40,000 sheep out of a flock of 45,000, Ben Ohau lost 33,000 out of 50,000 and Richmond saved only 300 sheep from a flock of 20,000. It was hardly surprising to see an English skylark lying frozen in the snow by the road. Large numbers of introduced birds are often killed in snowstorms up here. This high basin in the mountains, where temperatures sometimes drop to 30°C below, is no place for birds, and almost all of them had gone to warmer regions for the winter.

Suddenly we saw the sight we had been looking for — a black speck moving in a small mountain tarn. As we came closer, we could see the glossy black bird, stepping elegantly about on its long pink legs, probing for food with its slender bill. It was a black stilt — one of the fifty or so left in the world. This tough little loner, apparently undisturbed by the harsh conditions, was to be the subject of our first hour-long *Wild South* film.

Of course, we could not have found the small solitary bird in this vast landscape without help. The birds are often several hours' travel apart. We had been led to the right place by Ray Pierce, who knows as much about black stilts as anyone.

His interest goes back to his childhood, when he was growing up in South Canterbury, and often spending family holidays in the Mackenzie Country. From the age of ten, he was keeping diaries and making notes on birds — especially wading birds. As a child, he did bird counts around lagoons in South Canterbury and remembers:

Waders caught my eye. They were approachable birds, abundant and easily observed because they are diurnal — and quite often you saw rare ones.

Black stilt country, Tasman River Valley. Photo Graeme Matthews

Ray saw his first black stilt as a boy, looking it up and identifying it in Moncrieff's field guide. It intrigued him that there were so few, and over the years seemed to be fewer. Later, at university, he specialised in ornithology, and went on to make the stilts the subject of his Ph.D. thesis. When our director met him, his thesis was completed, but he was still living in an old cottage near the head of Lake Tekapo, and was being funded to do further research into some of the threats facing the black stilt. Ray helped us throughout our filming because he felt that an endangered bird should be the concern of all New Zealanders, not just a few.

The first place Ray took our film crew was a small mountain tarn, so that the bird could be filmed at close range against a bleak snowy background, showing how it could survive in the harshest conditions. Next he took us to a more typical environment — a river delta near Lake Tekapo. There was snow down to the water's edge here too, but the camera would not show it because the birds were out feeding against a background of water. There were half a dozen black stilts feeding here, all quite a distance from each other. The delta was obviously a rich feeding area.

Our main reason for coming here was to film the feeding methods of the black stilt. Ray said the bird had utilised a remarkable range of feeding techniques for the conditions it found itself in. It would have been an Australian bird which arrived here, probably in a very different form, many thousands of years ago. Gradually over the centuries, the birds had evolved their New Zealand characteristics of shorter legs and a long, strong bill, as well as their distinctive black plumage. They became particularly suited to living in the shallow braided rivers, large and small, which were typical of New Zealand, and not found in Australia.

Ray identified a number of the feeding techniques which the bird had evolved. Plunging: when the bird pecks at the prey living on or near the bottom of the river (including fish). Snatching: when the bird aims its beak at insects flying past. Bill pursuit: when the stilt rapidly opens and closes its beak on prey it has seen on the water surface. Scything: when the bird holds its head down, and sweeps its bill from side to side through the mud, for small worms. Probing: when the stilt pushes its bill in under stones to catch fat larvae clinging underneath. Raking: when the bird sweeps its bill back and forth through fine shingle, and catches any disturbed prey.

No other stilts have so many different ways of feeding. As Ray said, "Scything is very unusual for stilts around the world, and yet our stilts do it quite commonly." Other techniques, such as probing and raking, are only possible because the stilt has an unusually strong bill.

It is largely because of the bird's versatility in finding every kind of food available that it can survive through high country winters, so our director decided we should begin our film by showing as many of these feeding methods as possible.

The first move was to get the camera set up in some sort of concealed position at the edge of the river delta. We had brought along collapsible plywood hides, but knew it would be bitterly cold out in one of these — even wearing all the winter gear we'd brought with us. Fortunately a more comfortable alternative suggested itself. We managed to remove the side window of our yellow van, then backed the vehicle down along the water's edge and set up the camera behind the open window. We congratulated ourselves on having created the ideal mobile hide, comfortable and roomy enough for everyone inside — director, cameraman and sound recordist. In these conditions we knew we should be able to get plenty of good film of all the black stilt's feeding styles.

Now began the long slow work of watching and filming. It was interesting to see how different feeding methods were used in different conditions. In good light, the stilts could see clearly enough to peck and snatch at small items. When the water went cloudy or the light began to fade, the black stilts would shift to scything and probing — catching the food by feel.

As it turned out, the only method we had trouble filming was a stilt catching a small fish. Ray had told us that the fish in the Mackenzie rivers are unusually large prey for stilts, so it seemed important to see one being caught. However for quite some time we had no luck. And then finally a stilt obliged and gobbled down a fish right in front of the camera. Unfortunately this took the cameraman by surprise. His lens was focussed on a different bird, and he missed the shot. Annoyed and disappointed, he hoped that another of the birds might decide to take a fish as well. To improve his chances, he asked the director to take over the trigger at the back of the camera, so that he could concentrate on manipulating the cumbersome telephoto lens at a moment's notice. His patience was eventually rewarded. "Roll it!" he ordered and the camera whirred. "Got it!" he shouted triumphantly, as the black stilt raised a dripping bully in the air, and chomped it down with his long thin bill — it was a good shot. But the director thought he'd said "Cut it!" and switched off the camera! Again the black stilt's manoeuvre went unrecorded. Fortunately another stilt ate another fish later in the day, and this time it did go down on film.

Now we had filmed all the techniques Ray had told us about, and our first filming trip was over. We left, greatly impressed with this tough and versatile little wader. It seemed to be the master of its environment, feeding easily in a harsh winter environment, when most birds were scratching to find enough to eat even in warmer regions.

The plan was to film the black stilt at all the seasons of the year, so our film crew came back in early spring, to watch the birds mating.

Back at the same river delta were two pairs of stilts. They had already begun mating, although it was still too early in the season for most other birds. It was obvious that the stilts had been untroubled by winter, if they were feeling confident enough to make an early start to breeding. Birds only initiate mating when their food supply is sure and all physical conditions are favourable for starting a family.

The black stilt pairs were in roughly the same area where they had been in winter, but they were much further out on the delta. We could no longer enjoy the comfort of our modified van-hide, which had served so well for filming shore-line feeding. Close-ups were needed and the birds were now so far away that they were a small target, even when magnified twenty-four times by the cameraman's 600 mm lens. We decided we would have to get one of our portable hides right out on to the soft mud of the river

Following page *Black stilt pair at nest, Tekapo River.* Photo Rod Morris

delta. This was no easy task, but with the help of a local trucking company, we obtained some lengths of rusty corrugated roofing iron, and used these to build a runway out over the soft mud. Boulders were shoved under its edges for support. At the far end of our makeshift jetty we set up the hide. It only remained to get the cameraman and his gear out across the deep mud, without upsetting either the jetty — or the birds!

Stilts are sharp-eyed observers, and extremely sensitive to any strange new items or persons appearing in their living area. We set up our rather obvious hide well in advance of using it, so that they would get used to its presence. The cameraman put the end of a bottle into the hole where the camera lens would be, so that the birds would get used to a shiny object pointing out at them. But now we had to get the cameraman in position without alarming the birds. As most birds can't count, the best bluff for this was to accompany him as a group, drop him off with his camera, then leave. The stilts seemed to assume that the entire group of intruders had arrived and left together, and didn't seem disturbed.

However the cameraman remembers what happened next:

I found the whole rusty platform slowly sank under my weight! The stones shifted in the mud, the camera sank below window level, and the stench of swampy mud filled the hide.

After a while the rest of us saw what was happening, and waded out and shoved more boulders under the edges of the roofing iron. Then the cameraman went on waiting for the scenes he wanted to film near the hide.

For hours he had no luck. Then a pair of black stilts mated right before the camera. The footage had been worth waiting for. With many creatures, the act of mating shows them at their most awkward and cumbersome, but not so with the stilts. It was as if they were performing a graceful ballet. Afterwards there was a ritual crossing of rapier-like bills, and the male spread one wing protectively over his mate, then moved out of the camera frame.

The rest of the crew could see nothing of this. Without the 600 mm lens, the mating stilts were just specks in the distance. However we had plenty to do watching what was happening on the river banks, and planning further film sequences.

Gradually other birds, which had spent their winters elsewhere, were returning to the Mackenzie Country. There were banded dotterels, and wrybills, with their unusual beaks bent to one side in order to poke under stones. But most noticeable to us were the other stilts — the pied stilts. The main differences in their appearance were that they had longer legs, and feathers patched black-and-white rather than pure black. They also seemed less spirited in their behaviour. Sometimes a pied stilt would land next to a black stilt in the delta, and the black stilt would fly at it in a squawking fury of wings and bill, making the yapping cry which gives it its Maori name kaki. In almost every skirmish the pied stilt shifted away and seemed to come off second best. The black stilts were much better fighters, yet somehow the pied stilts were the more successful species. Soon there were far more pied stilts than black stilts around the river delta.

Ray Pierce said that the pied stilts might be something like the ancestors of the black stilts, which had come over from Australia so many thousands of years earlier. But the pieds, which are so numerous now, came over more recently, over the last two centuries. There had probably always been the occasional pied stilt coming over, but for most of New Zealand's history they would have been unable to compete with the dominant black stilt species. Since European settlement, this has changed.

Black stilts, like many other species had found themselves facing conditions which made life very difficult. Changes were made to their preferred habitats. Many of the smaller braided rivers were channelled between steep and narrow banks, to make them more convenient and easily controlled for the settlers. The deeper water and steep banks were less suitable for black stilts.

Even worse was the introduction of predators. Black stilts had evolved patterns of nesting by the sides of rivers, close to their sources of food. But the river banks were now highways for rats, cats and ferrets. Black stilts and their eggs and chicks were very vulnerable. Already by the end of the nineteenth century, black stilts were disappearing from the North Island, and becoming more rare in the South. By the middle of the twentieth century, they had become confined to their last stronghold in the Mackenzie Country, where their ability to survive the harsh winter conditions gave them a slight advantage over other species. Even here, they were becoming very rare, and were soon only able to survive at all through intensive protection.

As the black stilts disappeared from the waterways, the pied stilts gradually moved in. They weren't dependent on braided rivers, which were a new environment for them, and they had learned to cope with predators in Australia. So their numbers increased until they replaced the black stilt as the common stilt of New Zealand.

Yet Ray Pierce said that, after many years of observing both birds, he still found the black stilt the more interesting.

The black stilts are often solitary birds, and you can see their individual behaviour coming out. The pied stilts often tend to be in big groups, and one is a bit like the other. I remember one character — a black stilt — who didn't mate for years and years. It would often feed quite early in the morning and get its quota — then it would get up to a few pranks. It would fly around, often very high in the sky, so that it was just a speck. Suddenly it would sight a target, fold its wings, and just plummet to earth. The target was usually another stilt, of any sort. Once I saw it coming down on some cattle. And once it came down at me. I didn't know it was coming until it pulled out of its dive and uttered this terrible call. I got one hell of a fright! But it was just playing one of its pranks.

Above all, though, Ray found black stilts most interesting because they had evolved in an unusual landscape. Braided rivers, such as those found in New Zealand, are found in only a few other places in the world, such as the Himalayas and the Andes. He said: "I admire them because they are so well-adapted to the old New Zealand environment."

We finished filming the mating of the black stilts, and the arrival of the other birds into the area. Then we followed the black stilts up to where they were beginning to establish their nests — in the upper reaches of the Cass, Ahuriri and Godley Rivers.

We wanted to follow one couple through the nesting season, so Ray looked out a pair who seemed to be thinking about making their nest in a location ideal for our filming — a place which also showed the extent of the work which was being done to protect black stilts in the Mackenzie Country.

The area was enclosed in a fence about one-and-a-half metres high, which was buried in the ground so that rabbits could not burrow underneath and let predators in. It had electrified wires around it that cats and ferrets could not climb up. This fence, modelled on fences used to protect osprey nests in Scotland, was built by a large number of Forest and Bird Society members, local farmers and volunteers. It surrounded an area of about twenty hectares, inside which black stilts commonly nested. Ray thought that if we filmed a pair here, we could be sure that the eggs and chicks were safe.

We all watched through the fence as our couple inspected the terrain and took their time about selecting a nesting site where food would be plentiful and close by. They would be confined to the site for three or four weeks, so they had to choose carefully to combine easy feeding with close surveillance of their nest. As Ray had hoped, they picked a place where the cameraman could film them without going right inside the enclosure. It was an ideal arrangement.

The couple were filmed throwing their haphazard nest together in a large heap. Then the female laid her eggs — four of them. We watched and filmed the parents taking turns at sitting on the eggs and feeding.

Then, one morning, the stilts were no longer there. The nest seemed to be abandoned. When Ray went inside the enclosure, he found that the nest had been attacked by a predator. This was a shock, as the area was supposed to be predator-free, but Ray said that all the signs indicated that a brown rat had got at the eggs. It was probably the only predator which could have got into the area. (Fortunately rats are not a major predator in the Mackenzie Country.)

The birds re-nested, but not in a place where they could be readily filmed. A more photogenic pair was nesting on the Tekapo River bed.

Again we watched them nesting. They were down by the water's edge, just where predators were most likely to find them. However, Ray helped us set up a network of predator traps throughout the nesting area. Within two weeks those traps had caught nearly a dozen ferrets and wild cats. The cameraman spent as little time filming as possible during the early stages of nesting, so as not to draw attention to the nest and endanger the black stilts. As a further precaution, the eggs were taken to an incubator at a Wildlife station near Mt Cook, and replaced with dummy eggs for most of the incubation period. The true eggs were returned to the nest when they were within a few days of hatching. Then we watched and waited.

It was just as the birds were sitting on pipping eggs and the cameraman was waiting in his hide, that there was more eleventh hour drama. The Mackenzie spring weather did one of its customary but unpredictable turnabouts. Black heavy clouds rolled in over the mountains, wind lashed the river into a fury, and a storm of sleet pounded the land, bouncing like buckshot off the grey river boulders. The cameraman kept on sitting in the

Black stilt. Photo Rod Morris

cold, cramped hide. The eggs were due to hatch any time now, and he wasn't going to give up at this stage — but the hours went by, and he found it hard to keep alert.

Finally it was all worth it. He found himself watching a most memorable wildlife scene. The mother stilt crouched on her nest in the midst of the sleet storm. The ice formed on her back, and trickled away at the edges of her feathers from her body warmth. Her eyes were half-closed against the sting of the sleet. Then, in the frigid morning light, she stood up, and a fluffy chick dropped from her underfeathers. A second one followed, and two new black stilts had made their entry into the perilous conditions of the Mackenzie Country. The cameraman was able to take a few shots of the fluffy speckled chicks in the cold air, before they disappeared beneath their mother.

Within hours they were keen to be off to forage for themselves. They seemed to be as hardy as their parents, and able to stand up to the harsh weather, although from time to time they'd return to nestle under their parents' feathers, out of the cold. We were afraid of spending too much time in the area over the next few days, in case our presence attracted predators. So we completed this part of the documentary by going up to the National Wildlife Centre at Mt Bruce, where a colony of black stilts are kept in captivity. The chicks there were filmed launching themselves into the water and learning to swim and find food.

It wasn't until the chicks on the Tekapo River were almost able to look after themselves that we went back to film in the Mackenzie country again. There was a scene we were anxious to get, which had been observed in the distance over and over again, just after the stilt chicks had hatched. A harrier hawk, cruising high over the grasslands, hunting for food for its own chicks, would fly over the black stilts' territory. The young stilt chicks might have been an easy target — except for the vigilance of their parents. A parent would see the hawk high overhead, give the chicks a warning yap, and take to the skies. The chicks, their fuzzy feathers still speckled for camouflage, would react to the signal and freeze — motionless and almost invisible. High above, the black stilt would fly furiously at the harrier, shrieking at him and dive-bombing him with the sharp rapier of his bill. And the well-armed hawk always turned to glide away in another direction and look for easier prey. We felt this showed how well-qualified the black stilt was to deal with his ancient and only seasonal adversary.

Now that the chicks were bigger, it seemed safe to try filming such a scene. But we found that the stilt parents thought life was safer too! They were no longer worried about harrier hawks in the same way, as if they knew their chicks could look after themselves. We had to wait a long time before a harrier came close enough to alarm one stilt parent and this gave us the film we wanted of the harrier hawk being driven away.

There was something else we wanted to film before leaving the Mackenzie Country that season: the different nesting habits of the pied stilts, and the advantages these gave them in dealing with dangerous ground predators.

They were still in the early stages of nesting, and Ray said this was their first big advantage. Because they mated quite a bit later than black stilts, there was more food about and most predators were less hungry. However they had a number of other advantages as well. Ray took us to a nesting area which was on a small island in a lagoon — safely surrounded by a moat of water which would keep most animal predators away. It was hard to see the pied stilts on their nests. Their patched black-and-white colouring broke up the outline of their shape and made a "disruptive camouflage". However perhaps their most important defence of all was their communal nesting. The black stilts were solitary nesters, and wandered about with their chicks quite on their own. The pieds had eleven nests occupying one tiny island in the lagoon. Clearly they found safety in numbers. A warning from one would set them all on the alert. We even filmed a member of the pied stilt community removing a broken egg-shell from its neighbour's nest and flying off with it, so that its white interior would not give away the location of one of the well-camouflaged nests.

What if a menace such as a ferret did get through all these defences? Well, a pied stilt reacted to our cameraman as it would to a predator, and so we were lucky to see what happened when a bird was alarmed. The pied didn't react to danger as a black stilt would, with a flurry of flapping wings and a loud noise. It was more devious and more effective. It feigned a broken wing and shifted further and further away from the nest area, making pitiful noises. It was obvious that a would-be predator would follow, expecting to make an easy kill on a disabled prey. However when the pied stilt had led its pursuer far enough away, it took to the air and went back home, leaving the enemy alone.

Clearly, the black stilt, evolving for thousands of years in New Zealand, had lost such techniques, because most of its enemies were birds which approached on the wing. There had been less need to deal with predators on the ground. In Australia, where the pied stilt had lived until recently, such predatory menaces had always existed, so the bird had ways of dealing with them. The recent introduction by man of rats and ferrets and cats had taken the black stilt by surprise. It was a simple case of not being able to teach an old bird new tricks.

We wanted to film the black stilt at all the seasons of the year, so our next trip to the Mackenzie Country was in high summer. This trip produced some film which surprised everybody. The high country is certainly a region of extremes.

The first surprise was the heat — day after day of relentless baking sun, taking the temperature up to 40°C. Water which had frozen solid in winter now dried up altogether. Vast areas of mud hardened and cracked till they looked like old porridge. The Antarctic had become a Sahara, and the stilts were now moving up to the coolness of mountain tarns — shallow lakes which accumulate in the cups of the alpine hills. We went to the best tarn of all, Homestead Tarn on Benmore Station. It was ideal for wetland birds because its bottom is not just glacial pebbles but muddy silt rich in insect food. And here we met Jim Sutherland, the manager of Benmore Station, and another sharp-eyed observer of stilts, who helped us greatly with his experience and knowledge.

Ray and Jim warned us what to expect, but it was still amazing to see Homestead Tarn. The scene was like a choreographed water-bird ballet: black swans, Canada geese, paradise ducks, banded dotterels and spur-winged plovers — and, of course, stilts. They came whirring in, splashing down, and setting the tarn in motion as they sailed round and round like some colourful rotating pinwheel. Few New Zealanders would ever imagine that such a festival of birds could be held on an isolated mountain tarn in the remote High Country.

Our primary aim was to look for the black stilts, and they were there — wading in the shallows of the tarn, probing their long bills into the mud, or running about the shoreline under the bellies of Jim Sutherland's dry and dusty sheep which had come down to drink. We counted the stilts we saw there and compared the number with an estimate of the total remaining population. Almost half of the world's black stilts seemed to have come up to this one tarn. We saw a pair with two black-and-white young, now grown old enough to fly. Perhaps this was the pair of chicks whose birth had been witnessed during the early spring storm? If so, they had made it in the face of all the dangers from the ground and from the air. Now capable of flying themselves, they had little more to fear — but we knew they were amongst the very few survivors.

The pied stilts were there too, and as usual in far greater numbers than the blacks. Once again there were squabbles over feeding grounds. With their longer legs, the pieds could easily have fed further out in the tarn than the blacks, but they pressed in towards the shallows for control of the same strips of water. The black stilts, displaying their characteristic spiritedness and aggression, flew at the invaders and drove them off.

But Homestead Tarn had yet another surprise. It was here Ray pointed out a third type of stilt. He said that, at Homestead Tarn, we were getting our most extensive panorama of today's stilt population. As well as the small scattering of black stilts and the larger crowd of pieds, there were many stilts which stood out as being different from both. They were black and white like the pieds, but the two colours seemed to be rather randomly patched, spotted and speckled. Ray said that early ornithologists had once thought these birds were another species, but his more recent studies of plumage indicated that they are in fact hybrids — resulting from the interbreeding of blacks with pieds.

This kind of cross-breeding may be the final challenge to the black stilts as a species. With the black stilt so few in numbers the males are increasingly unable to find a mate amongst their own kind. Even among the small group of black stilts left, the sex distribution is (as with several other endangered species) skewed in favour of male numbers. Although a black stilt male will normally mate for life with a black female — and does if there is one available — he now sometimes has to mate with a pied. The pied females seem to be attracted to black males, probably because of their aggression. The blacks get the better of pieds in any contest for territory, and as in most contests of this nature, the female stilts (of either species) invariably choose the winners. In evaluating the dangers to the black stilt, Ray places predation ahead in importance, but hybridisation now a close second.

Wrybill on nest. Photo Rod Morris

Following page *Pied stilts, Matahui Point.* Photo Brian Chudleigh

But the knife is cutting both ways. New Zealand pied stilts, through interbreeding with blacks, are now showing black stilt characteristics. They are developing longer bills and shorter legs than the cousins they left behind in Australia. If the black stilt should finally disappear from the Mackenzie Country, he will have left his mark on the pieds which succeed him.

Autumn was coming on as we began packing our gear at the end of our last filming trip. We were not the only ones preparing to depart. Cold southerlies were beginning to bring the chill message of winter with them, and many birds were beginning to seek other locations and climes as the season of ice and snow began to take over the High Country.

The last footage we shot was of those who were not leaving — a black stilt family, two black parents and two young, moving slowly against the bronze water of the mountain tarn in the late sun. Until spring came again, they would be alone in this vast landscape.

Every attempt is being made to save our black stilt in its pure form in its last habitat, the Mackenzie Country. Trapping, such as we had seen around the nest on the Tekapo River is now a normal part of the black stilt nesting season. Since 1981, the Wildlife Service has been carrying out a major trapping programme, although the traps require constant attention if they are to be effective.

The work Ray Pierce is doing now is closely connected with this programme. He has a contract with the Wildlife Service to find out just what the circumstances are in which predators put the greatest pressure on ground-nesting birds like stilts. Of course, the number of rabbits about is a major factor. Predators don't live on a staple diet of black stilts. All the black stilts left in the world would not make breakfast for a fraction of the predatory animals now roaming their homeland.

Rabbits in the tussock grasslands are the predators' main food, and if there are plenty of rabbits about, predators may not bother with black stilts at all. The research Ray is doing at the moment should make it possible for trapping to be done as efficiently and economically as possible.

Yet another way of trying to improve the stilts' chances is to remove their eggs to an incubator and replace them with artificial eggs until the real ones are nearly ready to hatch — as we had also seen during our filming. And attempts are now made to see that each black stilt couple *have* eggs to hatch, even if their own have been lost and their re-nesting has not been successful. The black stilt colony at the National Wildlife Centre at Mt Bruce produces more eggs than can possibly be hatched and raised to maturity in the confines of captivity. Eggs from there are often brought down to the Mackenzie Country, to be raised by black stilts in the wild. (Sometimes the process is also reversed, and eggs from the Mackenzie Country are taken up to Mt Bruce — as Ray Pierce says: "to keep as many genes flowing as possible".)

A recent incident of this kind became a national newspaper feature, under the headline "Rare Chicks Saved". Three black stilt eggs, produced on the native bird reserve at Mt Bruce, were incubated to the point of hatching, then flown to the

Pied stilt preening. Photo Brian Chudleigh

Following page Pied stilt and newly-hatched chick. Photo Peter Reese

Mackenzie Country. The eggs were put in a nest on a small islet in the Ahuriri River to be hatched in their natural environment. They all hatched successfully and were being successfully reared when the river was hit by its worst spring flood in several years. One chick perished, but the other two were saved by the foster parents — who almost miraculously transported them to safety across the racing waters. It showed once again that the black stilt, when confronted only by the kinds of danger it has known for many centuries, is a truly intrepid survivor.

Soon there is to be a new development. An aviary and captive breeding colony is being established at Twizel, in the Mackenzie Country, so that black stilt chicks can be hatched there, and released into the wild as soon as they can fend for themselves. This venture will no doubt bring new drama and excitement to the struggle for survival of this species.

Each method of management of the black stilt has its dramatic stories. One of the most memorable is told by Ray himself. It was just after the first of the two fenced enclosures had been completed, and he was anxious to see how successful it would be. Then it began snowing.

A pair of black stilts was nesting in the enclosure, and they had two young chicks that Labour Weekend. It was a really lousy one. We had a tremendous amount of snow — about fifty centimetres at the nesting ground. I knew that there were going to be problems, so I waded through the snow, and sat on a terrace to watch the birds. I could see that one of the chicks was missing and had obviously died, and the other one looked very weak — and the female bird had disappeared altogether. Later on I found her carcase. She must have died during the snowstorm. But the male stilt was still there. I wasn't sure what to do. If I took the chick away, the father might not accept it back again. But I made a decision to go in and rescue the chick, because I didn't think it would survive if I didn't.

I collected the chick, and put it inside my jacket to keep it warm, and took it back to my hut where I kept it in front of the fire for three days, in a covered box so that it couldn't see me — or my Labrador! I fed it on mayfly larvae from the river, which I caught in a little netting trap that I put in the water. It was eating about 3000 of these insects each day and keeping me really busy. When it ran out of insects it would let me know, because it would begin cheeping, just like a chicken. I had to keep on re-filling the bowl.

But it survived all right, and after three days, the weather had warmed up and most of the snow had melted, and I wondered about letting it go again. I went down to the nesting area, and surprisingly the father was still there, still aggressively guarding his territory, even though his mate had died over three days ago, and one of his chicks had died, and the other had disappeared with me. So I just let the chick go.

It was quite some time before I knew that it would be accepted. It wasn't until it suddenly got very cold again that both the father and the chick decided at the same time that it was time for brooding, and they just ran towards each other. The chick went bowling in under the body of the male, who then squatted down.

The chick was named "Lucky". It grew up, learned to fly, and was colour-banded so that it could be identified. Now it has mated with another stilt, and has begun nesting.

This is one of the success stories.

Every survival is a triumph for the black stilt. For many years its numbers were rapidly declining. Now, with all the management techniques which can be mustered (including captive rearing), the black stilts are just holding their own. Their survival is precarious in the face of devastating snowfalls, predator plagues and hybridisation. Unlike other more widespread species like banded dotterels and black-fronted terns, local declines cannot be offset by recolonisation from other areas. However there is still a strong belief that they can survive in their pure black form on the New Zealand mainland.

For people like Ray Pierce, the Mackenzie Country without its black stilt will have lost part of itself forever.

Chapter Five

Saddleback

Riding Out the Rats

WHEN EUROPEAN SETTLERS CAME to New Zealand, they saw plenty of saddlebacks in the bush. The birds were common in both islands, in slightly different forms: the North Island saddleback had larger orange wattles and a faint gold line along the front of its saddle, while only the South Island bird was chocolate-brown for its first year of life and given the name "jack-bird". In their adult form, though, the birds of both islands had orange wattles at the beak, and a distinctive orange-brown saddle splashed across the back. They were one of the three ancient wattle-birds of New Zealand.

The saddleback was a bright, active part of the bush scene, chattering away, and feeding noisily on grubs and insects which it pulled apart with its unusually strong beak. It was such a vigorous feeder that it was sometimes accompanied by fantails and white-heads which hovered below to catch dislodged insects. A nineteenth century description from the book, *Out in the Open* by T. H. Potts gives a vivid picture of the bird:

It usually announces its sudden approach by a shrill note unlike that of any other bird we know; it sounds like chee-per-per chee-per-per, *repeated several times in quick succession. No sooner is this call-note heard than the bird emerges from its leafy screen and bounds before the spectator as suddenly as harlequin in a pantomime. From these abrupt movements, or flying leaps, thus shrilly accompanied, it seems to perform a* role *of its own that appears almost startling amidst the umbrageous serenity of the forest . . . its glossy black plumage is relieved from sameness by the quaint saddle-mark of deep ferruginous that crosses its back and wings, the red caruncles add much to the sprightliness of its air; the observer will probably notice that its attitude is peculiar, or, in colonial phrase, "it had a queer set on it." The head and tail are kept rather elevated, the feathers of the tail take a gently sweeping curve, the bird looks as though it is prepared to leap, one more glance and it is away. . . .*

The saddleback's cheeky nature is enshrined in a Maori legend which also explains the origins of its unusual markings. The demi-god, Maui, fresh from his battle with the sun, asked the bird to bring him water. It boldly refused. In his anger, Maui seized the bird with his still fiery hand and flung it away from him, leaving an orange-brown scorch-mark across its back. The bird's shrill voice was echoed in its Maori name 'tieke' and the cries were said to be good or bad omens, depending on the direction in which the bird flew.

South Island saddleback. Photo Rod Morris

The noisy fearless nature of the bird was little help to it when European settlement began. Its habit of often roosting and nesting in holes near the ground became a danger, and also its distinctive way of roosting in tiny crevices where there was no escape from attack. The birds' fledglings also came to the ground after they left the nest, and moved around noisily while they developed strength in their wings. Saddlebacks were easy prey for predators. The birds were beginning to disappear from many places on the mainland even before stoats and weasels arrived. Their great enemy was the rat, which overran the countryside during the first years of settlement — Norway rats (or 'brown' rats), and ship (or 'black') rats, which arrived a little later.

The explorer, Andreas Reischek, described the horror of these rat plagues in late-nineteenth century New Zealand:

New Zealand, especially towards the sea, now swarms with these animals, introduced originally from European ships. They are a pest in the North Island, but round the Sounds of the West Coast I found them more numerous still. I shot rats of all colours, yellow-brown, speckled, silver-grey, brown, grey, and black. . . .

I regularly poisoned as many as I could. At night they kept me awake with their noise, knocking things down from the walls, gnawing at my stores, and digging holes round the hut. They dug up the potatoes in the garden and dragged them away. On one occasion I hung up poisoned bird-skins, but sure enough the rats climbed on the beams and gnawed them to bits. . . .

The tussock country near the Three Brothers swarmed with them, and they used to gnaw our boots before our very eyes. . . .

These rats are the great enemies of birds, and any bird living or breeding near the ground has but a small chance of existing. They play havoc alike with eggs and young, and even attack the parent birds.

Between Landing Bay and Northport I found a great birch tree quite undermined with rat holes. The bark had been gnawed away up to 50 inches above ground-level. All vegetation was dead on the tree, and the stink of excreta was strong. It took five months of shooting, poisoning and trapping before they showed signs of decreasing around camp. . . .

A little later the ship rat became widespread, climbing with agility around the trees, and attacking birds, as well as competing with them for foods such as insects and fruit.

The saddleback had no chance against such enemies. By 1870, it had gone from the upper part of the North Island, often disappearing long before the land was cleared for settlement. Farther south, the birds were also becoming scarce. By the turn of the century, just as people were beginning to realise the beautiful huia was almost extinct, they also began to miss the bright saddlebacks from the bush of the North, South and Stewart Islands. By the early twentieth century, the saddlebacks had gone from mainland areas. Mona Gordon wrote in 1938: "Only an island life can preserve this bird from extinction, where, almost at sea level, among vermin-free patches of bush, it can pursue its unsuspicious way, and bring forth yearly its limited numbers of young in unmolested quietude."

Fortunately, the saddlebacks did survive on two off-shore islands — one in the north,

Muttonbirder Marty McColgan. Photo Rod Morris

and the other at the extreme south of New Zealand.

A small population of North Island saddlebacks remained on Hen Island (714 hectares) off Northland. The South Island sub-species survived on the 800 hectares of Big South Cape Island and two adjacent islets, off Stewart Island. Here they flourished and multiplied to the extent that the land would support them. On uninhabited Hen Island there were not many visiting people to enjoy their companionship, but on Big South Cape they remained an important element in an aspect of Maori culture which had been flourishing there for centuries and still does today — the way of life of the muttonbirders.

Every year, about October, great flocks of sooty shearwaters (known as titi or muttonbirds), and petrels come in from the ocean where they have been living and feeding for months. It is their breeding time, and they will spend about seven months nesting on various islands, amongst them those known as the Muttonbird Islands — of which Big South Cape is the largest. Each year they return to the same burrows, mate, nest, lay their eggs and hatch their chicks. These chicks are a traditional Maori delicacy, and in March, when the birds have reached a good size, the muttonbirders begin arriving to harvest them. The season begins on April 1.

Marty McColgan, a muttonbirder on Big South Cape, describes the legal and traditional background of muttonbirding:

When Stewart Island was sold, the muttonbird islands were excluded from the sale. The right to take muttonbirds on them was retained by the Rakiura Maori. They are the only part of New Zealand which has remained under Maori law. The rights to catch muttonbirds there are reserved for certain families and their descendants. These rights go back traditionally for many, many generations.

Each family has the right to a certain area of land, a manu. They do not own it in the European sense of ownership, but they have the sole right to catch muttonbirds there between the beginning of April and mid-May. There are no limitations on the numbers of muttonbirds they catch, as long as each family takes only as many as they can collect, clean and preserve themselves in the traditional way. There are a number of modern developments, such as using modern transport and equipment, but the muttonbirders do not employ labour or process the birds in factories, so that although each family works as hard as possible and takes some thousands of birds, it is not enough to make much impression on the millions of muttonbirds nesting there.

The muttonbirders jealously guard their rights to the islands and no one else is allowed to go there without permission from all the people of an island. They make considerable sacrifices to keep up their traditional use of the island and for the rest of the year have to engage in some job which enables them regularly to go away for the six weeks of the muttonbird season. Part of the tradition is to look after the manu and preserve it as it has always been. As Marty McColgan says, "The old people looked after it for us — we should look after it for those who come after us." If a family decide they do not want to use a manu, they cannot sell their right, or pass it on to anyone else. The neighbours catch birds on that manu until the family with the inherited right decide to take it up again.

Because the islands had been held in these traditional Maori ways and looked after by families who cherished them through many generations, in the middle of the twentieth century they were much as they would have been before European settlement began in New Zealand. Big South Cape, as the largest of the islands, was the most striking of all. In particular, the bush and bird life gave an idea of what the mainland bush might once have been like. One muttonbirder said that the air always smelled sweeter when he got back on the island. Another, Jimmy Bull said, "It was like going back to New Zealand as it used to be — it was like a little paradise on its own. The numbers of birds we had there!" Another birder, George Skerrett, described the chorus of birdsong as "deafening". People described seeing seven different kinds of birds in a single tree, as a common occurrence — all native birds. There were very few introduced ones.

When European naturalists occasionally visited Big South Cape, they agreed that it was indeed a remarkable sight. One of them described it as a "remarkable bird island — probably the most spectacular in New Zealand and perhaps one of the most spectacular in the world."

There were tuis and bellbirds, fantails, kakas, red-crowned and yellow-crowned parakeets, robins, moreporks, and many others. As well as birds which could also be found in other places, there were three birds found nowhere else but Big South Cape: Stead's bush wren (the birders called it the "thumb bird"); the Stewart Island snipe; and the South Island saddleback — all elsewhere extinct.

The birds were very tame, and became more so as the season went on. Muttonbirder, Doug Frew, tells of having to stop his axe in mid-air, to avoid hitting robins which had jumped on to the log he was splitting. Children often used to keep the parakeets as pets. Perhaps, though, the sociable saddlebacks were the birds most important to the muttonbirders. A saddleback would often be found nesting in a basket, sleeping in a parka pocket, or tucked up in the inside of a ball of twine. They didn't hesitate to enter houses or work houses to add their company to a gathering. The Maori had never wilfully hurt or killed tieke, which had always been regarded with a degree of reverence, as well as affection — the bird was traditionally supposed to keep guard over ancient treasures as well as being a bird of omen. The people of Big South Cape knew that the South Island saddleback was found nowhere else but on their islands, and regarded it as their special bird.

All of this, though, was before the rats.

The story of Big South Cape is one of the worst in New Zealand's recorded natural history, although it is a story which happened over and over again in other parts of New Zealand.

Although the events at Big South Cape happened many years before our Natural History Unit was set up, it seemed that here was a chance to talk to people who still remembered them. We decided to record their impressions and re-create what had happened. The documentary was called "Island Eaten by Rats".

There had possibly been a few rats resident on Big South Cape since the late-1950s or early-1960s. Occasionally a muttonbirder would report seeing a rat, about that time, but then nothing more would be seen of it and everyone would forget about it.

The species of rat which had come ashore was *"Rattus rattus"* — the 'black' or ship rat — the most efficient predator of the three species introduced to New Zealand by man. These animals are powerful swimmers and climbers, and could easily have come ashore from fishing boats anchored near the island.

Probably over a few years, a very small number of rats gradually increased until they had a population base to expand from. Then, in late 1963 or early 1964, there was a sudden explosion in the numbers of rats on Big South Cape.

Before they came down for the 1964 season, the muttonbirders heard rumours of what was happening. Jimmy Bull remembers:

The first report we had was from fishermen. We had no idea what it would be like till we got down here. We thought there'd just be the odd rat. But the whole place seemed to be infested all at once. Everything the rats could eat, they ate. What they couldn't eat, they fouled and destroyed.

Even as the birders were bringing their supplies up to their houses, they met the rats on the track — big fat fellows, in good condition, with alert translucent ears and healthy yellow bellies. Some of them were said to measure 45 cm from nose to tail tip. Though they darted away in front of the newcomers, a glance behind would reveal them already back on the track.

On reaching their buildings, the muttonbirders were greeted with a sickening sight. The rats had been through everything. All of the previous year's supplies that could be got at had been ruined. The stacked mattresses had been riddled and pulled apart and nested in. Where wallpaper had been stuck up as protection against draughts, it had been stripped right down so that the rats could eat the flour paste off the back. When the muttonbirders went to bed at night, they could hear the rats scampering about like kittens.

Doug Frew remembers building an addition to his house at this time:

I've a ring of ferns around my work-house. The rats would just sit inside the ferns, sunning themselves and watching me work. But they'd always dart off just before I was about to throw my hammer at them. I think they could read my mind.

It was the impact on their possessions and life-style that the muttonbirders felt first. They felt violated. Before, they had always expected to find things as they left them. Now they had to learn to shut everything up, and not to leave muttonbirds hanging up outside, and to surround their houses with poison boxes to keep the rats away.

Then, just as they were beginning to adjust to these changes, they were shocked to realise the devastating impact of the rat infestation on the varied wildlife which had made the island so beautiful. There were all kinds of changes, some more obvious than others. It took a while to realise that the bats which had slept by day in caves in the cliffs were no longer there. Children could no longer go down and stare at the hordes of

Muttonbird. Photo Rod Morris

Following page *Forest interior, Big South Cape Island.* Photo Rod Morris

strange little pig-faced creatures hanging upside-down from the rock ceilings, and birders no longer felt the occasional brush of a bat's wing in the night. One species of New Zealand's rare flying mammals — the greater short-tailed bat — had gone for good. There was no longer a teeming insect life in the leaf mould under the trees, although it took a while to realise this too. The large green skinks and mottled geckos were no longer to be seen sunning themselves on tree trunks and door steps.

However none of these things were so important to the muttonbirders as the loss of the birds. Jimmy Bull remembers:

The cocky robin vanished almost overnight. The yellow-headed parakeet in all their numbers went very quickly. The weka went down. The morepork seemed to fade with the others. The little fantails and tomtits held their own. The bellbirds were very scarce.

Lost were the fernbird, robin, banded rail, snipe, bush wren — and saddleback. Big South Cape had finally become just like the rest of New Zealand.

The people were particularly concerned about the birds which they knew existed nowhere else but on this island. It was hard to tell at first how badly the bush wrens and snipe had been affected, because they had always led rather secret lives — but they did seem to be more scarce. However it was easy to see that the saddlebacks, which had been so much a part of life, were disappearing. There were still some adults around, but no longer any of the plain brown "jack birds" — the young saddlebacks. It seemed that the rats had been attacking the nests and eating the eggs and chicks.

While the muttonbirding was still going on, the people did not realise the full impact of what had happened. The rats had not been able to affect the aggressive muttonbirds much. Anyway, there were so many of these that if some were killed it was hardly noticeable. It was when the season was over and the muttonbirds had taken off and left the island that the people really felt the shock. As Jimmy Bull said:

The island was dead. There was no life. Before there were always birds all round the place. When the muttonbirds left the island, the island was dead. That's when we really began to take an interest in the birds — after they were gone. We didn't realise what we had here until it was gone.

Of course, the way Big South Cape had suffered from rats was no different from experiences in many other parts of New Zealand. Whereas time had healed memories of what had happened on the mainland, here the memory was still raw and painful. The people had lost something precious within their own lifetime.

As soon as they could, the muttonbirders notified the Wildlife Service, in the hope that they could save the birds that were left.

As they left Big South Cape that year, they hoped that the Wildlife Service might be able to save the snipe, bush wrens and saddlebacks, and remove them to other islands. Perhaps someday the rats would somehow be eradicated from their island, and the birds brought back where they belonged.

The news about the rat invasion reached the Wildlife Service in early 1964.

By a stroke of luck, a team of people had been working on ways of shifting the North

Ship rat, Rattus rattus. Photo Rod Morris

Island saddleback during the previous year. It had been a matter of concern for some time that these remarkable birds were confined to two small islands. Although they hadn't appeared to be in any immediate danger, there had always been the chance that one of the islands would be struck by an ecological disaster just as had now occurred on Big South Cape.

Much earlier there had been attempts to shift the saddlebacks but these attempts had failed. In 1925, an expedition comprising people from the Dominion Museum, the Department of Lands and Survey, and the Native Bird Protection Society tried to re-introduce several pairs of birds to Kapiti Island near Wellington and Little Barrier Island in the Hauraki Gulf. The men involved in the work did not know enough about capturing and moving birds successfully, and a number of birds died in the process. Those that did survive the transfer had little chance of living long, as the new islands had not been cleared of wild cats and rats. In 1949–50, there was another attempt to shift some saddlebacks from Hen Island to the nearby, predator-free Chicken Islands, which was organised by the newly-constituted Wildlife Service. This time stormy weather prevented the success of the transfer.

There had also been some attempts to keep saddlebacks in captivity, so that at least some would be safe from extinction, but it had been found that they did not breed well out of the wild.

However, during 1963, three men were experimenting with new methods of capturing and transferring the wild saddleback to new habitats. One of them, Don Merton, was a Wildlife Service officer, who would later be given special responsibility for endangered birds and who was to play an important part in many bird rescues. Another, Johnny Kendrick, was an electronics expert who was interested in recording and reproducing bird calls on the new portable tape-recorders that were becoming available. A third, Ian Atkinson, was a botanist who was interested in the plant foods birds and rats ate, and who had a special interest in saving endangered species. This team had been studying saddlebacks on Hen Island, and trying out ways of catching them in a new type of very finely-woven, almost invisible, mist-net which had been imported from Britain and Japan, They used bird-calls to attract the saddlebacks.

Don Merton remembers some of the problems they had:

I was sure that we should be able to catch the birds with a combination of mist-net and tape-recording, but it wasn't as easy as you might think. They're a particularly agile bird. They don't fly much, but hop and climb around the vegetation — a bit like monkeys. Mist-nets are designed to catch birds in flight.

We'd put up the net in a place where we were sure that we'd get them, but they'd go over the vegetation or around it, rather than cross the six-foot gap where the net was strung.

The saddlebacks are very wary birds, too. They can see very well — and often seemed to see the net, particularly if it wasn't in a very shady place, or was blowing in the wind at all.

Still, we tried and tried, and at last everything fell into place. We got the technique of luring the bird in with a tape-recording of the right calls, and used a decoy to attract the bird to a specific point.

We found that they had to be kept in aviaries when they were caught — they just died if they were kept in small cages for long. We also had to experiment to find out what foods they would accept (they were pretty adaptable in their diet) — and the kind of carry-crates they travelled best in. It was fortuitous that we'd worked out all these techniques just months before the muttonbirders reported the rats on Big South Cape.

A wildlife expedition including Brian Bell and Don Merton was taken down to the island by the Royal New Zealand Navy in the winter of 1964, with the object of saving the three species unique to Big South Cape — the bush wren, snipe and saddleback. The first task was to visit other islands in the area to decide which ones would offer a suitable alternative environment for the birds. The seas were stormy and rough so this was an arduous job in itself. The men often had to wait to get ashore and to be picked up. In the end they decided that Kaimohu Island and Stage Island were the best places to shift the birds to. Then the Wildlife men were landed with their equipment on Big South Cape, and began the work of capturing the birds.

Don Merton goes on:

First we had to assess the situation. At the northern end of the island, destruction was most advanced: the rats were running about the forest in broad daylight, and most of the birds had gone. But in the south, especially in some remote localities, we found good numbers of saddlebacks — and there were a few bush wrens and snipe, although they seemed extremely scarce.

We built an aviary and set about using our new-found techniques to catch the saddlebacks. We had no trouble catching eighteen for one of the new islands, and twenty-three for the other. Fortunately, they usually came in pairs — first the male would come, and then its mate to explore the source of the calls. But females were already very scarce.

The Stewart Island snipe were much harder to catch. It was a little like catching butterflies. We would advance across an open area in a line and flush a snipe. Then we would sneak up to where it landed with our hand-nets, and attempt to catch it as it tried to fly off a short distance once more. This procedure was often repeated several times until we caught it. But we saw and caught only three snipe, and one of these got away.

We caught Stead's bush-wren by holding mist-nets in the ferns on the ground, for the wrens seldom flew, but we had to be very quick to scoop them from the nets. They were so tiny that they would climb right through the nets and escape back into the ferns. We caught nine of the little bush wrens.

The problems in catching three different species of birds, show how fortunate it was that the earlier experiments had been made with the saddlebacks. Although the techniques for handling were similar for each bird, the capture methods for snipe were different. The Wildlife team might well have had trouble catching saddlebacks too, if these problems had not already been met and overcome on Hen Island only months before. But perhaps more significantly it was much easier to keep wild saddlebacks alive in the aviary than the other two species — and it was necessary to keep them there for some time:

We had to wait and wait to transfer the birds, because the winter weather was so bad and days at that latitude so short. Rough seas made island landings impossible much of the time. We spent the short winter days hunting for insects and berries to feed our birds.

The saddlebacks were the easiest. We knew from our experience in the north how adaptable they were, provided they had a big aviary. Up there, we had been given a lot of old Christmas cakes that the shops hadn't been able to sell. The saddlebacks loved these and especially liked picking out all the sultanas and raisins and cherries. On Big South Cape they liked fruit such as apples. Of course we gave them what live insects we could find. Some of them became very tame, and would come up and feed right out of a bowl held in my hand.

It was unfortunate that at that time we did not know so much about the foods for the snipe and bush wren. We fed the wrens on small insects, but three of them died. In the end, we held them in our hands and fed them tiny grubs and honey-water through an eye-dropper, and kept the rest alive that way. We didn't know enough about the snipe's diet either — and would have a better chance now, because we've experimented with the Chathams Island snipe. They need a large and constant supply of live insects day and night. We didn't know that then. The two snipe died before the boat came.

And so the Stewart Island snipe became extinct.

It was a relief when the boat came at last, and Don Merton and the others could begin the work of moving the birds to their new homes. First, a group of saddlebacks was taken to Stage Island. The seas were rough, but not too bad, for this first liberation. However the weather was getting more and more squally. The Wildlife party was afraid that the Navy would not want to approach Kaimohu, the other island in worsening seas. However the Navy felt it was better to get the job finished and get away:

We wanted to release the birds as soon as possible. Fortunately the commanding officers of the naval patrol launch Mako *said, "We'll get them ashore one way or another" — so off we went. There was a big sea running. When we reached the lee of Kaimohu Island there was a four-metre-or-so rise and fall. It was too rough for a dinghy. So the skipper tried coming in towards a shelving rock — trying to get close enough so that the team leader, Brian Bell, could step ashore. The skipper brought the boat in half a dozen times, but there was a big side-current, and each time he was about two metres off. At last he came in so that the bow rose briefly above the rock; and Brian stepped off.*

Then we rigged up a kind of bo'sun's chair between the shore and the ship, and put the boxes of birds on that, and got them ashore.

Brian let the birds go. He tied the rope around himself, and we dragged him back to the boat through the icy surf. Then we were off home.

It was a question of waiting until summer to see if the birds would survive on their new islands. Fortunately they did. Even the bush wrens were seen the next time the Wildlife officers visited their island — although they did not appear to be breeding. Gradually they died out. The species known as Stead's bush wren — the last of three subspecies of bush wren unique to New Zealand — also became extinct.

However the transfer of the saddlebacks was a success and they were soon flourishing and breeding in both their new homes. In two years, there were enough to transfer to

Stewart Island snipe — now extinct. Photo Don Merton

Following page *Stead's bush wren — now extinct.* Photo Don Merton

other small islands, so that their chances were even better. Each year, Wildlife officers have gone back and redistributed them on many of the suitable small islands and now, twenty years later, there are about 500 South Island saddlebacks on a dozen small islands, although they soon became extinct on Big South Cape Island.

Soon the same process was being carried out with the North Island saddlebacks, and they were moved to a number of islands in their area. The most spectacular success was on Cuvier Island, where twenty-nine birds were released in 1968 and there are now more than a thousand. The lighthouse keeper on Cuvier Island sees them coming right into his garden and around his home.

For the time being, tieke is safe.

The saddleback story must be one of the world's few conservation success stories, where an endangered species has been reinstated in the wild. The story of Big South Cape is a tragic one — described by botanist Ian Atkinson as the "worst biological disaster to have affected an island in New Zealand during this century." Yet much good came out of it. The rescue of the saddleback showed for the first time anywhere in the world that, with foresight and planning, an endangered species could be brought back from the brink of extinction. People also began to take rats more seriously as predators, and to look at how New Zealand's other precious islands could be safeguarded against them.

In 1983, after these events had been played out, it was decided that the story was so important that it should be told for television — even though it is no easy task to re-create the past on film. Of course, if it had been human history, we could have put actors in costume and made models of old buildings. But how do you re-build the natural history of an island?

We began by talking to many of the people involved, to build up a picture of what had happened. Then we had to patch together film from here and there to bring that picture to life for the television screen.

To show how life on Big South Cape might once have been, we went to Stage Island and filmed a few of the birds which had once been so prolific on Big South Cape — including the saddlebacks which had been shifted there. On Stage Island, we also filmed the insects, wetas, beetles, skinks and geckos which had vanished from Big South Cape. For the robins and yellow-crowned parakeets, we had to go to tiny Poutama Island, as there were none on Stage Island. Although neither of these islands had the abundance and diversity of bird life that Big South Cape once had, gradually — as different shots were put together in the editing room — an image of what it must have been like was created. Of course, even then some species were missing. For the snipe, we had to go to a near relative in the Chathams. For the little bush wren there was nowhere to go, for everywhere else rats had killed them off much earlier.

For our film of the rat, we used a wild ship rat in a variety of locations. As it was carried around, it showed a remarkable ability to survive. One day it got out of its terrarium in the boot of a car. At first it was assumed to have escaped. But eight days later, the rat was discovered, still in the car, fit and well after having had no food or

Wildlife officer removing South Island Saddleback from mist net. Photo N.Z. Wildlife Service

Previous page Morepork. Photo Rod Morris

water for all that time. It had built a comfortable and secure nest deep inside one of the car seats. Despite traps being set, another three nights passed before the rat was once again back in captivity. It showed just how easily rats might have stowed away on fishing boats to be taken to Big South Cape, and what an indestructible enemy the saddlebacks and other birds had been up against.

For the film of shifting the saddlebacks, we used some old film, shot in 1967, of saddlebacks being shifted from Stage Island to other islands. The techniques both of shifting and filming would have been much the same as they were in 1964. We filled this out with some new film of birds being shifted the season we were making the *Wild South* programme, as this still happens most summers.

For some better close-ups of saddlebacks feeding we went to an aviary near Invercargill. There it was impressive to see the fearlessness of the saddlebacks when a cat came right up to the cage. They just ignored it. Don Merton said that, some years earlier, when the saddlebacks were first taken to this aviary, he saw much the same thing. A cat began prowling along the protective netting on the side of the aviary. The saddlebacks had never seen a cat before, and they immediately dashed down to take a closer look, following it along as closely as they could – even when it tried to catch them!

Our film crew learned a great deal in the process of recreating the story of Big South Cape Island for *Wild South*. Most of all though we learned from the people who told us their stories. We learned from the muttonbirders, what it had been like to live in an island paradise, and how the horrors of the rat had changed that. And we learned from Don Merton about the very first steps in developing techniques to rescue endangered species. As Don Merton described the experimental expeditions of the early 1960s:

Every waking hour we were deeply engrossed in the whys and wherefores of what we were going to do and how we were going to do it, because the challenges were formidable. Now much of this is routine, techniques have been developed — and everyone's more used to this kind of thing and can switch off at night and have a game of cards. In those days it was really urgent and vital that we find ways of overcoming obstacles — and succeed.

The year when the saddleback was saved was important, not only because of the rescue of that unique and irreplaceable bird, but because it showed to the world that an endangered species *could* be saved, and some of the ways of doing it. The techniques developed at that time have since been developed further for other species, not only in New Zealand, but all over the world.

In 1971, the International Union for the Conservation of Nature's *Red Data Book* included a special green page for the entry on the South Island saddleback — denoting a species which had become less endangered. It was the only green page in the book. At the foot of the entry it said: "Those New Zealand ornithologists who planned and executed this remarkable rescue of a species indeed deserve the congratulations of all conservationists."

Only one bird species in the world at that time had been saved unequivocally by direct human intervention, and that was tieke, the New Zealand saddleback.

Saddleback in full song. Photo Rod Morris

Chapter Six

Kakapo

The Old Night Parrot

FIORDLAND, IN THE SOUTH-WEST corner of the South Island, is the least known corner of New Zealand. Here age-old secrets remain where no human has set foot.

In the hush of a Fiordland night, when black space fills the forests and valleys, non-human sounds expand the darkness. The muted roar of avalanches and waterfalls from far ridges, the occasional croak of the morepork and the squeal of a kiwi. And in certain unpredictable years, a throbbing sound of drums — the low rhythmic boom of the kakapo.

There can be no doubt that man is attracted to mysteries, and in 1974 a team of scientists set out into the dense, mist-shrouded forests of Fiordland to search for the strange giant bird, as green and secret as the place itself. The bird's colours had been described as "rich moss green, shading to light yellow green on the underparts", but "mottled and freckled all over, like shadow and sunlight" — except that this bird seldom saw the sun. The Maori name for it was 'kakapo', meaning 'parrot of the dark', because it shunned sunlight. Its sun was the moon. Maori lore told of its strange nocturnal rituals, when birds made their way to secret playgrounds, and danced for hours, uttering deep-toned cries which travelled for miles through the night air.

Sometimes the birds were even snatched up from the hypnotised rapture of their dance by Maori hunters who found the kakapo very good to eat. The large flightless birds were also caught with Maori dogs or snares on their feeding grounds. The meaty flesh was roasted in hot stone ovens or in gourds full of boiling oil. Warm and fragrant feather capes were made out of the sweet-smelling moss-green skins — skins more valuable than mink and sable have ever become. There is a Maori adage to describe someone who is never satisfied: "You have a kakapo cape, and you still complain of the cold."

Although kakapo were once found all over New Zealand, by the time Europeans arrived in the early nineteenth century, they had become scarce throughout the warmer North Island where the Maori population was concentrated. In the South Island they had retreated to the central spine of mountains along the western coast. Always mysterious and secretive, they became difficult to find and see. Those Europeans who did manage to observe them, however, were fascinated by the kakapo. Sir Walter Buller wrote in his *History of the Birds of New Zealand*:

Kakapo displaying. Photo Rod Morris

This is one of the very remarkable [bird] forms peculiar to New Zealand, and has been appropriately termed an Owl Parrot. Dr Sclater refers to it as "One of the most wonderful, perhaps, of all living birds . . ." In all the essential characteristics of structure it is a true Parrot; but in the possession of a facial disk (in which respect it differs from all other known Parrots), in the soft texture of its plumage, and especially in its decidedly nocturnal habits, it betrays a striking resemblance to the Owl tribe.

A later observer, Richard Henry, commented on the large size of the "owl parrot":

I think it is the largest and the only one out of the great family of parrots that cannot fly. Probably its ancestors could fly, and like the rails, came here on the wing; but the absence of enemies on the ground, and the abundance of food, allowed the muscles of the wing to degenerate and those of the leg to develop, until now they are fairly good runners and their wings are only for ornament. . . .

As Henry believed, and later scientists have confirmed, the kakapo is the heaviest parrot in the world, weighing up to three and a half kilograms — although when its ancestors first flew here, they may have been no larger than the budgerigar. Over the centuries, in the safe, rich forests of New Zealand, amongst an abundance of food, the kakapo gradually grew to a gigantic size for a parrot.

However, the kakapo's days were numbered, and Henry wasn't slow in realising why:

. . . just now the "lords of creation" have imported ferrets and weasels that prey on all such things that sleep on the ground and, as kakapos cannot be expected to learn in a day what their race had forgotten for thousands of years, the chapter of their history is in all likelihood coming to a close.

Fortunately they have many friends, and the New Zealand government takes a kindly interest in their affairs, and has appointed two reserves and men to put them out upon islands.

Richard Henry was one of those men. He was given the job of shifting kakapo and other rare birds to the first bird sanctuary — Resolution Island, in Dusky Sound, Fiordland. With the help of a muzzled dog, he managed to track many of them down, in spite of their secretive nature:

Some of them rest on the ground under ferns during the day, but the great majority prefer to take up their quarters in hollows and dens in the moss among the roots and trees . . . So well does their colour accord with the yellow and green of the ferns that it is impossible to see them unless they move. Of this they are well aware, and often keep perfectly still even when within arm's length.

With the help of his dog, Henry managed to catch about 400 of the large birds in the wilds of Fiordland, and painstakingly ferried them by small boat to Resolution Island. Here he thought they would be safe, as the island was free of predators. However, after six years' hard work, he made a heart-breaking discovery: "August 28 (1900). I am very sorry to have to say that I saw a stoat on Resolution." The sanctuary, so laboriously created, was no longer safe for the kakapo and kiwi which he had taken there. Stoats had swum across the Sound.

During the twentieth century, kakapo became extremely rare. Most people were beginning to wonder if there were any left. Then, in 1960, two officers of the Wildlife

Service were tramping the Tutoko Valley above Milford Sound, with historian John Hall-Jones, when they found fresh signs of kakapo — fallen feathers, and the whitish balls which the birds leave hanging after munching leaves. Five birds were subsequently trapped in the area, and sent to the Mt Bruce Native Bird Reserve for study. They all proved to be males, but formed the basis for limited kakapo research until one by one they died.

Searches continued in other areas and a few more birds were discovered, but there was no attempt at serious research or management. The discovery that kakapo had not yet died out aroused new interest, and Fauna Conservation Officer, Don Merton, proposed that further explorations in Fiordland be undertaken urgently to answer important questions about kakapo. How many more were left, if any? Where were they? How did they live, and were they breeding? It was going to be expensive to send such expeditions into these rugged mountain regions, which were largely accessible only by helicopter. Still, in 1974, the money was found, and the project given highest priority over all New Zealand's endangered species programmes.

Consequently a team under the leadership of Don Merton was sent to search for kakapo in Fiordland. One of the members of that expedition was a young Wildlife trainee, Rod Morris, who later joined the Natural History Unit.

Coming into Fiordland by air, the region thought to be the last redoubt of the kakapo seemed poetically designed for it — a lofty Shangri-la landscape of mist-shrouded inaccessible valleys, cascading mountain torrents, steep and rugged ridges and remote, mountainous rainforest. Here the secrets of this strange bird began to unfold.

As an inconclusive report had been received of kakapo sign in the Esperance Valley, the search of 1974 began there.

Don Merton was looking for areas which Richard Henry had once described as "kakapo gardens". These are areas where the beech forest is broken by small patches of disturbed ground — often through avalanche. Such patches are sheltered by higher trees, and are like natural greenhouses where five-finger, hebes of various species, wine-berry, bush-lawyer, tutu, *Coprosma* and other quick-growing berry plants flourish. According to Richard Henry, kakapo were often to be found feeding in such gardens.

When he had found such an area, Don went down after dark, and settled down to listen. Much later that night he heard a single parrot-like "kraaark" nearby. The following night, he waited in the garden again, and this time he had a little cassette recorder with him. He could hear what may have been a kakapo close by. It skirted round him, only a metre or two away. Then it "kraaaked" and he pushed the button on the tape-recorder and managed to record the latter half of the call. But it was very faint. Back in camp, with Johnny Kendrick, who specialised in recording bird-calls, they dubbed and re-dubbed the faint signal on a professional tape-recorder until they had a louder version of the call, which they played back to the bird down in the garden. Every time the kakapo heard the tape, it responded vigorously and they recorded its varied responses. There were ear-splitting shrieks and screams, sounds like a braying donkey,

Following page Kakapo country, Sinbad Valley, Fiordland. Photo Rod Morris

and a crowing rooster, grunting and squealing like a pig, a purring sound almost like a cat when it came close — as well as the parrot-like "kraak" they'd expected. These first tape-recordings are still the only recordings of many kakapo calls.

When the calls were played back to it, the bird seemed very interested in the intruders in its territory. One night it climbed up a nearby tree to inspect, and could be clearly seen in silhouette against the night sky a few metres above. It was a thrilling moment for Don.

The next step was to trap the bird. Don had permission to take three pairs of kakapo out of Fiordland to a safe off-shore island. (At that time it was not known that kakapo do not form pair bonds.) Several walk-through traps were set, but it was nearly two weeks before a bedraggled old male was captured, which was christened "Jonathan". He was put into the make-shift aviary, where everyone looked at him in awe. Don Merton said: "You know, we could be looking at the last live kakapo left on earth!" The bird had a strange perfume, not unlike freesia flowers — perhaps a way of marking out territory. At first everyone was worried about how this very private bird would take to being kept in the strange surroundings. For days it wouldn't eat, but eventually relaxed enough to munch on berries, and then began trying new foods such as apples and kumara.

Now the aim was to prove that he *wasn't* the last bird left. The party worked further down the valley next night, and directed the tape-recorded kakapo call up on to the sheer valley walls. Almost miraculously, there was an instantaneous response from high on the western wall. The next day, signs of a kakapo were found there, and a dog used to find the bird. It proved to be smaller than Jonathan, as females were supposed to be, so it was christened "Jill". The two were sent up to an island sanctuary in the Marlborough Sounds. There old Jonathan eventually disappeared, and Jill died. An autopsy then revealed that the second bird had been misnamed. "Jill" was a male.

This first trip had shown that kakapo still existed, but it was on the next expedition the following season that there was a major break-through in understanding kakapo behaviour. Late that year, 1975, another male bird was found in the Esperance — a very large and hearty one. He was named Richard Henry in honour of that doughty old pioneer in kakapo conservation, and was shipped off to Maud Island in the Marlborough Sounds, where he survived for seven years until stoats reached the island, when he was transferred to Little Barrier. As no other birds could be found in the Esperance, the party then moved on to the Tutoko. While hunting for kakapo there, a broad track was found, with the tussock cut on it as if by a scythe. The track led between two perfectly round bowls, about 40–50 centimetres across and 12 centimetres deep.

This was just like something which Richard Henry had described:

. . . we found a hill-top near the south east corner of Cascade that was nearly covered with pathways and "scratching-holes". The ground all round looked as if there had been an attempt made to clear it of ferns and sticks, and every root was bitten and peeled as if they had tried to remove it.

I walked all over it and had a long look at it, and somehow the idea was forced on me that this was their playground or ball-room, and that if I could come here in the season with the eyes of a cat I might learn something of their social forms and customs.

Kakapo "booming", Fiordland. Photo Rod Morris

That night observers lay in the tussock, and heard the sound of "booming" coming from the bowls. This strange kakapo behaviour had been mentioned by Richard Henry and others, and in Maori lore. Henry recorded:

Months before the appointed breeding season the male is developing an air sac in his throat, which he can puff up like a drum, and which may act like a sounding board to assist in making the curious drumming notes in spring.

This rhythmically repeated "boom" was apparently the means by which the male kakapo attracted a female during the years chosen for breeding — years which were said to be irregularly spaced, perhaps depending on the plenitude of the plant food required for the successful hatching and rearing of chicks. It was the most unlikely and surprising sound ever to come from a parrot — a deeply resonant call, something like a fog-horn. The sound was emitted in a regular monotonous rhythm of about one boom every two seconds, in choruses of 20–50 booms, repeated for many hours. It was suspected that the bowls, generally flanked by a natural reflecting surface, assisted in the projection of the sound across the dark valleys. The sound could be heard for several kilometres.

Looking around the next day, more kakapo tracks and bowls were found, although most seemed long-disused. It looked as if many males must have once boomed together "in concert" to attract the elusive female. Don Merton immediately suspected this as "lek" courtship behaviour, though it was known in no other New Zealand bird. Later, when he reported the discovery to the well-known British bird behaviourist, Edward A. Armstrong, he learned that, although this form of behaviour is shared by about eighty other kinds of bird in the world, it is practised by no other parrot — so yet another of the kakapo's extraordinary characteristics had been uncovered.

A mysterious Maori tradition, described by Elsdon Best, and once treated as something of a myth, began to make sense. Best wrote:

A most singular circumstance in connection with the Kakapo and its doings is the custom, ceremony, or amusement of the Whawharua. As is commonly known, the Kakapo is a night bird, and during the day it remains concealed in rugged and precipitous places. At night, however, the birds come forth and collect at their Whawharua, which is a common meeting place or playground for all birds which belong to that peculiar tribe . . . Having collected, every bird, with one exception, goes through a strange performance, by beating its wings on the ground and uttering its weird cry, at the same time forming a hole (pokorua) in the ground with its beak. . . . Each Whawharua has its leader, which is known as the Tiaka. During the above performance the Tiaka keeps walking round the outer edge of the Whawharua, presumably acting as a kind of sentry, and does not join in the picnic. At dawn the Tiaka leads the flock back to their hiding places. This Tiaka is said to have been always a small bird. . . .

From what had now been discovered, it was clear that the smaller bird must be the female, with a number of interested males all performing to her from their bowls or courts. Thus, Richard Henry was not far wrong when he described the area he saw as a "ballroom".

So far it had only been possible to *hear* the booming in the dark, but Don Merton was anxious that the display performed in the darkness should also be seen. During that Christmas break, he arranged to borrow a light-intensifier-scope, or *zeniscope* — a recent military invention which could amplify light by up to 50,000 times. The light-intensifier gathered together available light — moonlight or starlight — and intensified it to form a greenish image of what was going on in the dark. With this piece of equipment, it should be possible to watch the kakapo booming without disturbing them — and especially to see if any female was present to visit the male.

Don Merton went back to the bird which had been booming before Christmas, and watched it briefly for the first time, but unfortunately the booming ceased after only a few nights. So Don sent his team to other valleys around the area to see if they could find other booming birds.

In Sinbad Gully, beneath Mitre Peak, Rod Morris and volunteer Richard Gray set up hides near track and bowl systems belonging to two different kakapo there. Both systems showed fresh signs of having been actively used. Later Rod wrote down some of his experiences. The first description is of the lower of the two systems:

There were hours of waiting, cramped in our little hide in the dark, silent night, watching the green-lit circle of view through the zeniscope. Then into that green-coloured world waddled a kakapo, rocking along on his thick feet. His giant proportions came as a surprise — almost three times the size of a kea, and leaving footprints nearly as large as a human hand.

He entered his bowl, and tidied it with his hooked beak — then settled into the curved dish as a hen settles into the dry dust of a fowlyard. He crouched, and fluffed his feathers out, and then, very quietly, he started humming: "Mmmmmmmm . . . mmmmmm . . . mmmmmmmm. . . ."

He then tucked his head down into his deep chest and blew himself up so that he looked like a balloon covered in feathers, and started the booming sound — which was just as strange and powerful as we'd heard previously when sitting out in the dark.

It looked exhausting work, and the booms went on for hours. I kept wondering when a female would arrive, but our hopes of this gradually faded as the nights passed. No one knew then, but there are probably no females left in all the mountains of Fiordland. This booming of the males is a sad and futile exercise.

Richard and I kept watching night after night. One windy night, the old male left his bowl, and tried to mate several times with a fallen tree branch. The leaves were being lashed around in the wind, and he seemed to be excited by the movement. What would have happened if a female had arrived? This was something no one knew.

On another night though, higher up the ridge at the other track and bowl system, Rod was lucky to see part of the answer.

I was watching the second bird from the hide further up the ridge. This kakapo had become somewhat accustomed to human company, and was increasingly approachable. One night a visitor to the hide had held out some cabbage to the bird and it had nibbled at it. It was also beginning to fool around the hide, and looked as if it was going to try to make a new bowl underneath our hide platform. And so one night I climbed out of the hide with a weak, red-filtered torch, to have a better look. The bird didn't seem to mind at all. It came right up to me, climbed heavily up on to my shoulder, and sat on my head! It was a great weight, with a fearsome grip on my scalp, and at first I was apprehensive. Finally it jumped down, and wandered back to its bowl.

Then, to my amazement, the bird spread its wings like a butterfly, and began waving them slowly. He clicked his bill and started swaying from one foot to the other. He lowered his head, and rhythmically treading the ground on alternate feet began slowly moving towards me, coming closer and closer until he was only about six feet away. Then he began turning around, still coming towards me, only now he was walking backwards! He rocked from one foot to the other until his tail touched my boot and then just stopped, with his back towards me, his head lowered, and his wings widespread — they were intricately-patterned like the wings of a moth or the tail of a peacock.

For a while he just stood there, wings outspread — I was obviously expected to make the next move! I didn't. Finally the kakapo turned around and gently tested my boot with its beak before climbing up on to my shoulder again.

For the rest of the night that kakapo followed me wherever I walked in its track and bowl system, and for much of the time it danced. It was incredibly sad to see it dancing hour after hour, and to realise that there must be no female for it to dance to. It must have been the unexpectedness of seeing another living thing on its track and bowl system, after waiting so long, that made it dance in vain. I noticed however, that if I left the track and bowl system it lost all interest in me.

It didn't like other observers coming to watch on subsequent nights, either, and eventually tried to bite and claw them.

There was another expedition into a nearby area in 1976, when Rod had an even more eerie experience of the mating dance of the kakapo. This time it was in the Transit Valley.

It was the end of the booming season, but one bird could still be heard at night. We knew where the track and bowl system was and so I set up a still camera, camouflaged with moss by what seemed to be the bird's main bowl. We were due to leave the next day, but I was hoping that maybe, at the eleventh hour, I'd be lucky enough to get a coloured photograph of a kakapo booming.

I settled in behind a log in my sleeping bag, and waited and waited — then sometime after midnight, I fell asleep. About four in the morning I woke up, and something wasn't quite right. There were strange soft noises all around me in the dark. I turned on my torch to find great wings were opening and closing less than a metre from my face. It was another kakapo. It turned around towards me, and kept on dancing. I got up and took a great many photographs. As with the bird in the Sinbad the year before, this one followed me as faithfully as a dog around its track and bowl system for over three hours. At 7.30 a.m. I had to leave to be flown out, and the bird was still dancing in the grey dawn light as I left.

These were exciting revelations of kakapo behaviour in Fiordland in the 1970s. Some of the mysteries surrounding the bird were being uncovered for the first time. But it also seemed to be a dead end. The hopeful kakapo searchers were seeing the last days of a dying race. Only about eighteen birds were discovered, scattered over the mountain ridges — a few booming males, vainly competing for the attentions of females who seemed already to have vanished. Until early this century, Fiordland had been the stronghold of this unique bird, but now it was all but extinct.

Then, in 1977, came a break-through. South of Fiordland, on an uninhabited part of

A wild kakapo examines the photographer's boot. Photo Rod Morris

Stewart Island, the Wildlife Service located what seemed to be a healthy population of kakapo. Again it was Fauna Conservation Officer, Don Merton, who, following up reports, planned the search to find them. He set up four two-man teams for the operation, and within six hours of their helicopter landing, each party had found clear signs of kakapo.

In the following days a diversity of track and bowl systems was found. They did not go straight along ridges, but extended in all directions, winding around trees and other obstacles, for unlike Fiordland, this was more of a rolling landscape.

Then came the impressive discovery at the southern end of Tin Range — soon to be called "Arena Ridge". There were no less than twenty-three occupied track and bowl systems, or courts. These showed clearly the male kakapo's courtship methods. Each bird had its own track and bowl court, but they had grouped their systems together into an "arena" so that they could boom together. Many such courtship arenas had been found in Fiordland, but all were long-disused. This one looked quite fresh. (It was later found that some males would travel many kilometres from their normal home ranges to display there.)

The whole kakapo world was obviously more alive and flourishing in Stewart Island than it had been in Fiordland. But how had the birds survived so well, and remained undiscovered for so long? It seemed intriguing that the area of greatest kakapo concentration coincided on the map almost exactly with an area of the Tin Range where miners in the 1890s had staked out 144 claims and worked the alluvial deposits for tin and tungsten. Yet there were no records or accounts of the tin miners ever seeing or hearing the kakapo. This was odd, as lone workers of this kind had usually shown considerable interest in any kakapo they came across. As one writer said: "Unfortunately the Kakapo too often fell victim to the early gold-digger, prospector, saw-miller, and road-maker; in Otago during the construction of a certain road, the Night Parrot was slaughtered in great numbers, one bird making 'a plenteous meal for two men'."

Why had the tin miners never noticed the kakapo? It was another of the many mysteries surrounding the bird. One theory was that there had been very few birds on Stewart Island at the time. The miners had burned off the trees to get at the bare earth, and with time this had produced a regeneration of new scrub adjacent to the more mature forest. In Fiordland the kakapo had shown a strong preference for areas of regeneration and sub-alpine scrub for feeding, close to older beech forest for refuge. Perhaps the area of the Tin Range was now like a huge "kakapo garden" and the miners had set up the conditions for the bird's later resurgence in that area.

Whatever the explanation as to how they got there, the population of kakapo now discovered was unlike anything seen in recent times. The very first bird seen on Stewart Island looked different from the Fiordland birds. It had paler colouring, so that at first it was thought it might be of a different sub-species. Then Don Merton realised that it was a young bird — probably not more than a year or two old — whereas all the birds found in Fiordland had been old. After some study, a population of around 200 birds was estimated to exist on Stewart Island. Although no females were found at first, it was felt

Male kakapo. Photo Rod Morris

Following page Male kakapo dancing, Fiordland. Photo Rod Morris

that they had to be there somewhere. Indications were that this was probably a healthy kakapo population, which should be quietly monitored for a while.

And so over the next two years, the kakapo work on Stewart Island was carried on by a number of Wildlife research scientists — mapping, counting, analysing foods and droppings, and monitoring behaviour by placing microphones in track and bowl systems, and tracking kakapo movements. Gradually a mass of scientific data was accumulated. However by 1979 an essential piece of data had still not been found. Nobody yet knew whether there were any females.

In 1980, a concerted effort began to try to find a female. A Wildlife team came in, accompanied by dog-handlers and their muzzled dogs. A television news team also came to cover the story, and shot film which would later be used in our *Wild South* programme.

It took a while to learn how to use the dogs. At first the handlers tried working them in a line, but this proved to be a social outing for the dogs, who frisked with each other and found nothing for days. Then the handlers decided to work the dogs independently, and this had better results. Three kakapo were found in one day.

The first six kakapo caught were all males. Everyone was getting worried. However the seventh kakapo was different from any others seen — it was smaller, greener, narrower in the head and more pinched in the face. Don Merton was back in camp when Gary (Arab) Aburn arrived with something in a sack. Arab said, "I think I've got a female!"

First Don checked the trailing edges of the tips of the primary wing feathers. On male kakapo these are patterned, but a parrot expert in Britain had told Don that in some parrots there was often a difference in markings between the sexes. Don had checked this in museum specimens and on the few female skins available, and had found what he believed was a subtle but consistent difference. The wing tips on female birds were blank. And so they proved to be on the bird which had just been found. This, combined with other features described by nineteenth century authorities (notably Richard Henry), led Don to confirm that a great moment had arrived. A female kakapo had finally been found — the first to be seen in at least seventy years.

The female bird was held until measurements, droppings and photographs could be taken. Then she was released. However the search for females went on. Altogether about five females were located that season — and more would be found in the years that followed. Everyone was jubilant, and it was a turning point in the kakapo story.

In 1981, kakapo boomed again on Stewart Island, and in Fiordland. In Dunedin the first *Wild South* series had just gone to air, and we wanted new stories to film.

A film crew went down, and our cameraman's hide was set up at a place where a kakapo was expected — near a track and bowl system with all the signs of fresh use. We had special night-vision equipment, so that filming could be done without disturbing the birds.

There was a long wait. Then, just before dawn, the kakapo arrived, rocking his heavy body into the circle of the view through the zeniscope. He settled into his bowl and began panting, with some slight visible movement in the nostril pads. Then he produced the first sound — a *"tcht — tcht — tcht"*, a bit like someone operating a bicycle pump. He swelled until he was almost spherical, buried his beak in his chest, and the deep resonant beats of the booming began. For the first time the unique performance was recorded on film. We kept wondering if the call of the male would at last be answered by the appearance of a female, but this was not to be.

The next two nights, the kakapo appeared only briefly — and the next night not at all. Everyone wondered whether our 'alien' human presence might have driven the bird away. Then on the fifth night, the kakapo came back — and something new and fascinating happened. There was another sound — a sort of *"ching-ching"*, which was like a sharp cry, almost like an animal caught in a trap. The call moved on the hill, and went on for about half a minute, part of which our sound recordist managed to record.

The effect on the male bird was dramatic. He suddenly stopped booming, as if startled, then resumed again with a kind of obsession which could not be disturbed. He seemed to be absorbed in a trance-like rapture of booming. All over the ridge, the persistent booming seemed to spread like tribal drums. The ringing *ching-ching* cry was not heard again, but we were all convinced that we had heard the rare answering call of the female kakapo — and later this was confirmed by Wildlife scientists who heard the chinging on a number of occasions on Stewart Island, and agreed that the sound was probably made by an approaching female.

We still had hopes of seeing her appear at the bowl during our remaining nights there, and dreamed of filming the legendary mating dance. However she didn't come, and we imagined that she might be circling the bowl, disturbed by our scent. It seems now that a female will never come to a bowl which is being watched unless very elaborate precautions are taken.

On our last night our crew decided to see if the kakapo would dance to *us*. Rod Morris was directing his first film. He decided to attempt to repeat his previous experiences of watching dancing birds.

While the cameraman waited, he began moving around and talking quietly at the back of the hide, and then shifted around to the front. The kakapo seemed completely oblivious to his presence, and just kept on booming. To make the bird take notice, he shone a torch towards it — a ruse which had interested the males in Fiordland. But at this the kakapo simply moved around behind the bush, away from the light — and kept on booming.

However hard we tried, we could not entice the bird to dance for the camera — probably because he was not suffering from the hopeless frustration of the males in Fiordland, but had good reason to think a female would eventually come. Time ran out, and we had to leave Stewart Island with the kakapo still having kept the secret of his mating dance from our prying television cameras.

This season still had one great secret to share with us though. A few weeks later, the news came that the Wildlife people had found two kakapo nests with chicks in them.

Following page *Kakapo bowl, Arena Ridge, Stewart Island.* Photo Rod Morris

Naturally they didn't want a television crew there while the chicks were still very tiny and vulnerable. Kakapo chicks are confined to the nest site for many weeks and lack any means of self-defence. They are also left alone for much of the time. So there was enough danger from predators without any additional activities drawing attention to the nest. However Don Merton said that if all went well, a television crew might be able to go and film the chicks later in the season.

When the chicks were almost three months old and ready to fledge, he thought it was safe for us to come.

The crew arrived on Stewart Island about 3 p.m. one afternoon and were taken to the nest of a chick named "Snark" (after Lewis Carroll's "The Hunting of the Snark" — because the Wildlife people had had to hunt so hard to find him; they'd called his mother "Alice", because she kept disappearing down the nest hole to feed him). We could stay only three days, so we worked hard to set up the hide and filming and sound-recording gear before nightfall. As we worked we could hear Snark down in his hole from time to time. One minute everything would be quiet, then there'd suddenly be loud grumbles and grunts coming out of the hole in the ground, as if the young bird had woken up and bitten his foot or banged his head. Then he seemed to drop off to sleep again. Don said that Snark hadn't once come out of the hole yet, but was probably getting pretty close to leaving the nest as he tried constantly to climb out. There was no sign of his mother, Alice, but Don said she was roosting nearby, and would come back to feed Snark once or twice during the night.

By dark, everything was ready, and the cameraman settled down in the hide to wait, hoping to catch a glimpse of Snark's beak appearing out of the hole to collect his meal. But there was much more than that to see. That night we had extraordinary luck. At about ten o'clock, Snark decided to climb right out of the burrow for the very first time and take a look at the world.

The camera filmed him climbing up over the step of the cavity and out on to the ground outside. He craned his neck and looked all around, took a few wobbly steps — then slipped and fell back into the nest. Half an hour later, he was out again, stretching his wings, testing things with his bill, grabbing at a little bush and playing with it almost like a kitten. He was a fluffy creature with the face whiskers of an adult, so that he looked rather like a little walrus. When his mother came to feed him, we saw that he was already larger than she was.

The cameraman had thought he'd be lucky just to see Snark being fed in the nest, but he was able to film Alice regurgitating a thick berry porridge into his bill as the chick stood on the ground outside.

Poor Alice looked skinny and bedraggled, as if she'd been run off her feet trying to feed him. As kakapo have no pair bond, she'd had the sole responsibility of bringing back food for her chick. We had a glimpse of just how hard her life must be when Don took two of us down a track to watch another kakapo mother collecting food for her chicks. (It was impossible to watch Alice, as she went somewhere away over the ridges.) When we got to the feeding ground, it was amazing to hear the heavy flightless kakapo mother moving around near the top of a twenty-metre rimu tree, collecting berries. (She had a radio transmitter attached to her back so that her movements could be followed.) While she was still up there, we began heading back to camp. But, a little over 30 minutes later, Don, listening to the radio transmitter, said that the female kakapo had already arrived back at her nest — a kilometre from where she'd been feeding. She must have run past us in the dark. And probably soon she'd be off making another trip. It was an incredibly hard life, for she would make two trips during the night — a total of at least four kilometres over rough, boggy and hilly ground.

During the three nights we were there, Snark became steadier on his feet, until he could move quite a distance from his nest. At first he stayed within a few centimetres of the nest hole, but on the third day he was going three to four metres away, and exploring around trees where we could no longer see him. As he was going out of range of the camera, we didn't feel quite so bad about leaving him when our time was up.

That last night, our cameraman filmed a satellite flashing across the sky. It made us feel that, although the experience of seeing Snark was cause for celebration, there was a sad side to the event. Man is pushing further and further into space, exploring new planets. It's easy to forget about the habitats that are being destroyed and the creatures that are being displaced in our wake. Creatures like Snark.

Our scriptwriter wrote these words to go with the image of the chick emerging on screen. "On a June night, Snark finally emerges for the first time. But the night he has chosen to come forth is the wrong night. . . . in the wrong century. It's no longer a land of birds out here for the young night parrot."

By the time our film was presented, we knew that Snark's life would not carry on in a simple, natural way on Stewart Island, because in 1982 had come the cat scare.

Wild cats had roamed Stewart Island probably since the first human settlement at Pegasus Bay in the 1860s. No one knew how much they had harmed the kakapo because no one knew the kakapo were there. However in 1981–1982, sixteen cat-eaten kakapo were found. Over fifty per cent of marked adult birds were being killed each year. Cats may have been attracted to the area during the booming period. Possibly scientists were inadvertently to blame, in that they cut tracks to get to the kakapo country, which also made it easier for cats to get there. The holocaust could have been the work of a small number of cats, or even one rogue cat that had got the taste for kakapo.

No one could say why it happened, but the effects were disastrous. In 1977 when the kakapo were first found on Stewart Island, there were estimated to be about 200. By 1982, the number had shrunk to less than 100. Arena Ridge which had thrilled observers with its many track and bowl systems, now supported three or four males. The revival of hope which had come with the discovery of the Stewart Island breeding population turned to fear.

Many cats were destroyed, so that soon the danger was lessened. But Don Merton knew that complete eradication of all cats in the area was not feasible, and that it might not be possible for the kakapo population to survive and recover in their presence.

Kakapo breed slowly — as slowly as elephants — nesting only every few years, and raising but one or two chicks.

In an attempt to enhance survival of chicks, he proposed a fostering programme. Some birds were believed to hatch more chicks than they could raise. Fertile eggs and healthy chicks could be shared amongst available mothers, so that as many would reach maturity as possible. However this didn't always work. In 1985, Snark's mother Alice laid four infertile eggs, and Don gave her a fertile egg from another mother. Alice sat on the egg like glue until it hatched, and then began busily feeding the chick. But after a week, it disappeared — almost certainly the work of a rat. Tiny, noisy, helpless kakapo chicks are sitting targets for many introduced predators.

Like Richard Henry and others, Don Merton is convinced that large off-shore islands free of mammalian predators are the kakapo's only long-term hope for survival in the wild. Snark is now living on Little Barrier Island, with a number of other kakapo put there in 1982. A second island population is soon to be established on Codfish Island, which is currently being prepared. This island, off Stewart Island, is now clear of predators. It is only 1480 hectares in size, and could become a miniature Stewart Island where kakapo can prosper unmolested.

Although there are not many kakapo to colonise this new home, it is amazing that there are any at all. As Don Merton contends, the kakapo has more in common with the dodo than any other bird he can think of: it is flightless; nests on the ground; is herbivorous, and must walk great distances to get its food. It lays tiny eggs, which hatch small helpless chicks, which take months to become independent. The dodo became extinct three centuries ago, whereas there are still probably about eighty kakapo left in the world — in Fiordland, Stewart Island, and Little Barrier. This is an amazing feat of survival. As Mona Gordon has written: "In bird history the kakapo's story stands alone, even in the land that produced the lost moa."

In the dark of some future night, a television crew may yet go to the kakapo's new island sanctuary and film its magical mating dance — although with the kakapo no one should count on anything, even if the bird should survive and flourish.

After the trip to film the booming kakapo on Stewart Island in 1981, Rod Morris made one last attempt to get film of a bird dancing and later described what happened:

My last hope of filming a kakapo dancing was a dream which didn't come true. I went into Fiordland by myself to see if I could find a lone male who would dance for me. If I was lucky, I was then hoping to take a television crew in to capture the scene on film. I knew it was probably too late in the season by now, but it might be years before the kakapo boomed again. I had to try.

I ended up by climbing a rock face and spending the night, without a tent, on a steep ridge, near a track and bowl system which had been freshly used. It seemed the last hope of seeing or hearing something. But no bird came, and at five in the morning I was driven out by a terrible storm, and had to climb down the rock face in the dark. It was a crazy thing to do, and something I'd never want to repeat. Still, after it was all over, I felt glad in a way that the kakapo had decided to keep that last secret.

Kakapo. Photo Rod Morris

Chapter Seven

Black Robin

The Robins' Return

EARLY IN 1984, NEW ZEALAND'S newspapers carried the following report.

Special: "Old Blue is missing, assumed dead. News of the disappearance of the bird known as the great-grandmother of all existing black robins on the Chatham Islands was reported by a Wildlife Service party which is attending the new breeding season.

One can only assume that the 14-year-old robin who almost single-handedly brought her breed back from the edge of extinction has finally died," the Minister of Internal Affairs said yesterday.

"Old Blue," named from the colour of her leg-band, was certainly the most famous individual bird in New Zealand, known to most school children and people in every walk of life who had followed her career with concern. But what was the story behind this creature whose life and death made international news and was the concern of Cabinet Ministers?

She was a small wild songbird, with sparkling black eyes and matching coat — one of the rarest birds in the world. Her life began about 1970 on a tiny rock stack known as Little Mangere Island, in the Chatham Islands cluster, 850 kilometres east of New Zealand's South Island. At the beginning of her story, she and a few others were holding out in a tiny forest which crowned the 200 metre high basalt fortress like a medieval castle. They were the last of their species and had been isolated here for over 80 years. Now their citadel of trees, buffeted by gales, undermined by burrowing seabirds and strangled by tough vines, was falling about them. Food was running out, and their young were diminishing in number.

The black robins had been considered rare ever since they were first discovered by a European naturalist in the 1870s. They were found only on the Chatham Islands. Although similar to the North and South Island bush robins, they were completely black, instead of dark grey and white. All of the New Zealand robins are thought to be descended from the same brightly-coloured Australian ancestors which colonised this country thousands of years ago; probably good flyers when they arrived, in their new land of abundant food and few predators, their wings degenerated and they developed longer legs as well as distinct colouring in the different islands' populations. In the nineteenth century, the black robins were apparently wide-spread on the larger islands of the Chathams. But by the end of the century, with the introduction of cats and rats,

Little Mangere Island. Photo Rod Morris

and the clearance of forest and scrub from the larger islands for farming, the black robins were found only on Little Mangere, and their numbers were very low on this tiny island.

In 1972, an American scientist, J. A. Douglas Flack, working with the New Zealand Wildlife Service, was assigned a research project on the black robin, and visited the bleak and formidable heights of Little Mangere. His project involved studying the unique population of black robins, as well as the New Zealand mainland robins, to obtain knowledge that would be useful in managing the black robin. The first step was to catch and colour-band the robins so that their survival, movements and breeding performance could be monitored. The bird who became known as "Old Blue" was the one given a blue leg-band.

Flack was surprised when he arrived on the remote island to find that the population was far smaller than earlier guesses had indicated — only about eighteen birds at the most. It is quite likely that they had been close to this level since late last century, since it was apparent that the extent of forest habitat and space on Little Mangere was sufficient to sustain only about five breeding pairs at any one time. While Flack was conducting his study, between 1972 and 1975, he observed that the habitat was deteriorating, and the robin population was rapidly declining. There was high mortality during the breeding season, and alarming reproductive failure. He became increasingly aware that unless something was done there would shortly be no birds left to study.

There seemed to be a number of reasons why the robins' habitat was degenerating. Firstly, a man-made change had disturbed the already delicate environment. In the 1960s, part of the forest and scrub had been cleared to create a helicopter landing-pad, extending up to the cliff-edge. There was a crayfishing boom in the Chathams at this time, and a number of helicopters were plying the area. These were hired in off-peak times to fly poachers to the top of Little Mangere Island, where muttonbirds were taken illegally. The helicopter landing-pad created an opening in the bush, through which the mighty "Roaring Forties" winds buffeting the rock stack now rushed unimpeded.

Tens of thousands of muttonbirds, breeding on Little Mangere, had riddled the soil with their burrows, loosening the roots of the trees. Now exposed to the strong winds, and with no firm footing in the soil, the old trees began to fall, and the robins' essential forest canopy was disappearing. At the same time, *Muehlenbeckia* creeper, a rampant vine, gained an advantage in the deeper soil of the forest clearing. This vine can be a blessing or a curse. When it was confined to the edges of the forest, at the cliff-tops, it had formed a dense screen to ground-level, keeping out rain and wind. There it was good nesting cover for small birds, and a source of caterpillars and seeds in season. But once the forest had been disturbed and opened up, the vine became more vigorous. As it got in amongst the trees, it began smothering them, gradually covering the canopy, and blocking out light inside the forest. It also acted as a sail, catching the wind, and this helped to topple the big trees. The essential elements of food and shelter were disappearing. In his three-year study, Doug Flack saw the black robin population plummet from eighteen to nine birds.

Clearly the end was in sight, but Doug Flack was uncertain about what should be done

Two black robin fledglings. Photo Andrew Penniket

or how. There was no way to regenerate the habitat on Little Mangere in time to save the robins. The only alternative was to move some robins to a healthier environment. But would removing some of them spell doom to those left behind? How should they be moved? How many should be taken? How old should they be? When should they be shifted? Where should they be put? Doug Flack could raise these questions and more but he couldn't answer them. He was a researcher, not a management expert.

An eleventh-hour meeting of decision-makers in the Wildlife Service was held in Wellington in late-1975, when the black robin population had just fallen to nine. There the crucial question was discussed: should some sort of removal be attempted in face of all the risks? The decision against it would have been unanimous, but for one voice — that of Don Merton, who considered that any further postponement would be fatal to the species and that the decline had already continued for far too long. Having lost his case, Don went on to other work with kakapo in Fiordland. However while he was there the nine black robins became eight, and the decision-makers had a worried change of heart. They contacted Don, and instructed him to proceed to Little Mangere for black robin management.

By the time he and his team arrived in 1976 on the top of that precipitous rock in the Pacific, the eight had become seven — and of the seven only two were females. The black robin was now the rarest bird in the world. Only a miracle could save it.

Don Merton had tackled many challenging tasks, but the one ahead of him now was daunting. The risks were fearsome and all eyes were on the endeavour. Everyone was waiting apprehensively for news of the attempt to save the tiny, black powder-puff of a bird with the quick bright eye and spindly legs and endearing personality. At this stage there was no longer any room for mistakes.

The decision had been made in Wellington to transfer the birds from Little Mangere to a sister island, Mangere Island. This was close, being separated from Little Mangere by a narrow gap of only 100 metres — but it was far from being an ideal refuge. Although it was a much larger island, it was unfortunately a barren habitat for birds over most of its surface. However at the end of the island furthest away from Little Mangere, there was one place which could provide a suitable home for a small number of black robins. Here a precipitous scree of huge boulders fell steeply down to the sea. A small forest, about the size of the forest on Little Mangere, had survived the ravages of fire and grazing by sheep, in the shelter of the high rocky wall. As forests go, it wasn't much; many of the trees were deciduous, losing their shelter in the crucial winter months; but there was much dense regeneration in and around the older growth. Although it wasn't a good prospect in the long run, it seemed the best solution in an emergency.

The first problem was to shift the birds from the top of Little Mangere across the ocean gap to Mangere Island. This was such a difficult operation that a team of seven Wildlife people was needed to shift the seven birds. The robins had to be netted, put into safe carry-boxes, and carried on the backs of climbers down a sheer and dangerous face of crumbly rock, 200 metres high. The precious cargo then had to be carried in a small dinghy to the northern end of Mangere Island.

The authorities back in Wellington were understandably cautious in dealing with the rare black robin, and had given permission to shift only one pair. However, after sizing up the situation, the men on Little Mangere decided that in spite of the risks, it was necessary to act more boldly, and shift the lot, for if left the birds would undoubtedly die. If the operation went wrong, as it so easily could, the responsibility was entirely on their shoulders. This was to be the first of many such worrying decisions.

Don Merton today recalls his fears and misgivings about those hazardous journeys:

Climbing down the cliff was one thing. It took the best part of an hour to get down. Then there was the boat trip around to the far end of Mangere. When I think of it now the risks were not so much the boat ride itself, in a Lancer dinghy, but the getting ashore at the other end — because it's not very often that one can land on that boulder beach. It's a terrible place to land. There's almost always a big rise and fall, and no nice steep little rock you can get up against and step ashore. It's just a steep grade of big slippery boulders.

Knowing what we know now about that island — we've spent months there and we know it very well — how on earth we landed all those birds through that surf without the loss of a bird or a person, or even a broken leg, beats me.

It was just as the work of shifting the black robins was beginning that Television New Zealand came on to the scene. News of what was going on in the remote Chatham Islands had reached Dunedin. The daring rescue mission was obviously a great New Zealand wildlife story which should be recorded on film. Permission to land on the islands for documentary purposes was sought and granted. A television crew finally reached Mangere Island, after an eight-hour trip by fishing boat — just in time to witness the arrival of the first bird ever to be transferred.

The cameraman still remembers the thrill of being there with camera running when the first black robin was released on Mangere Island:

When we filmed that very first robin being released there was just the sound man and myself, Brian Bell (the leader of the expedition) and Tony Billing (a Wildlife trainee). We saw the box lid open and the bird fly out. Tony stood back and said, "Oh Corker! Corker! Corker!" And Brian called back to Little Mangere on the radio to tell the boys up there that it had all gone well. He said to them, "He gave a little warble as he flitted up over the bush!" These two sayings have been enshrined and used time and time again, over the ten years of the black robin project, whenever anything goes particularly well.

Having filmed the successful arrival of the first bird on Mangere Island, our television crew was keen to get over to the top of Little Mangere, to watch the birds leaving. We got our chance when a member of the Wildlife team came across to Mangere Island for supplies. He offered to guide us up the tricky climb on the cliffs of Little Mangere, so that we could film the next robin transfers. We were grateful that the Wildlife people seemed to accept our presence as part of the whole complicated operation, and not an intrusion. They, too, thought it important that a wide audience should see what was going on.

It wasn't easy getting up the 200-metre cliff face with television camera, assorted lenses, tripod and sound recording gear. Some ropes helped on the worst sections, and near the top there was a wire ladder, but at some points there were no such aids. One jutting rock ledge required that the climber let go of any rope and hold on to the overhanging shelf while edging around it, and the rock was so unstable that it looked as if it might break off (and bits often did). We were all glad when that climb was over, and we had reached the top of Little Mangere, ready to film the next robin capture.

The captures were made as early as possible in the morning, so that the robin would get its journey over and have plenty of time to settle into the new forest before dark. We set up our gear, ready to begin filming. The cameraman filmed the mist net being raised to ensnare a robin, and the sound man recorded the calls being made to attract the bird. Then there was quite a long wait. Fortunately, when a robin heard the calls, it was anything but shy, and flew readily into the mist net. The cameraman filmed all this, and the Wildlife men moving towards the net. But he did not attempt to show the robin actually in the net. It was a tricky business handling the bird and he did not want to get in the way. Later, though, the cameraman was fortunate to see a stray blackbird caught in the invisible strands of the net, and as it was the same colour as the robin, we were able to use a distant shot of this to illustrate that part of the story.

Once the robin was caught, it was filmed being carefully placed in one of the cool, dark carry-boxes Don Merton had designed, and being carried down the cliff to the boat. It was interesting now to see how the Wildlife people reacted to the strain of the events. The cameraman recalls watching the transfers:

I remember the nerves that came over them once they had that real black robin in their hands. Those guys changed, knowing what they were entrusted with and what was ahead of them. I recall Dick Veitch. Once they had that box with the bird in it, and secured it on his pack, he was just a different person. It was the awesome responsibility of getting that precious bird down that cliff and across.

Next a pair of birds was captured, and carried down together. Don Merton was heard to say to the trainee carrying them, "Now remember, you've got half the world's breeding population of black robins on your back, so be careful!"

Five birds were safely carried over — two pairs and one solitary male. Then it was decided to leave the remaining two males on Little Mangere, as they could not contribute to breeding that season in the very small habitat, and were best out of it.

Back we all went to Mangere Island to see how the birds were settling in. Surprisingly the pair bonds had changed when the birds were shifted. A solitary male had been chosen as the first black robin taken to Mangere, to minimise the risk in the initial transfer. His brief time alone on the new island seemed to give him a confident mastery of the new environment which impressed the first female to be brought over. She joined him and deserted her first mate, who was now left alone. However he was joined by the second female to come over, and in turn her former mate was left as the loner.

The black robins seemed to be accepting their new home, but the Wildlife people obviously still felt some anxiety as they watched the birds settling in. What if they didn't stay in the bush, but moved along to the other end of the island and headed back to Little

Wildlife officer carries a pair of robins down cliffs on Little Mangere Island. Photo Rod Morris

Mangere, guided by homing instincts? With no trees on the way, and vulnerable to hawks and skuas, they would not stand much chance of getting there safely. Even if they did make it "home" they wouldn't last long back in that degenerating environment.

Our television crew had to leave shortly after the transfers so we didn't see for ourselves what happened next. However when we came back later in the season, we found that the birds had settled in well. There had been a few problems. For instance all over the floor of the forest on Mangere Island was a thick layer of leaf litter full of the insects and grubs which black robins like to eat. But there had been no such litter in the old forest on Little Mangere, and the robins did not know how to search for their food there. The Wildlife people had to teach them, by walking through the forest and scratching down into deep pockets of leaf litter to uncover all the good food. However, the robins learned quickly and were soon doing this for themselves.

Best of all, the black robins were breeding in their new home. By the end of the season, Old Blue had successfully raised a daughter. The other female and her mate were alive and well, too, although their breeding efforts had not been successful. The lone male had disappeared. As the new young female needed a mate, and the environment of Mangere Island had proved suitable for the robins, the Wildlife Service now brought across the last two males from Little Mangere.

All the black robins were together on Mangere Island, but there were still only seven. And that winter a lone male died.

Then there were six black robins!

We closed our *Wild South* film, "Seven Black Robins," with this news. Despite the desperate ending, it had been an exceptionally satisfying documentary to make. The film seemed to capture people's imaginations. We were frequently asked what was happening to the black robins.

Unfortunately the news from the Wildlife Service was not good. Although several chicks were raised in the new forest on Mangere Island over the next few years, some of the older birds from the original transfer died of old age. In 1978, the number of black robins had dropped to five. In 1979, there was another birth and another death, and the population was still only five.

It was obvious that further help was needed, and Don Merton was sent back to Mangere Island to try to work out what should be done. Before long, he was proposing a plan as risky as the original transfer. It meant introducing the technique known as "cross-fostering". At this time the technique had never been used in New Zealand (although it has since been tried with other species). It was only in its experimental stages overseas, and was being tried with a few large birds such as the Whooping and Sandhill cranes in North America, never with small bush birds. The proposed programme involved removal of the robins' first clutches of eggs to induce the birds to lay again and increase egg production two or threefold. Usually a black robin would lay just two eggs, and spend the next three months trying to raise perhaps one chick. However if the bird lost the first clutch of eggs, it would usually lay another clutch, and if it lost

Black robin about to be released. Photo Rod Morris

Following page Don Merton with black robin. Photo David Merton

those, possibly even produce a third lot. If eggs were removed and given to a foster parent of another species to hatch and raise, it might be possible to double or even treble the number of eggs raised in a season.

The foster parents which Don thought might be best for the black robin eggs were Chatham Island warblers — friendly little bush birds which abound on Mangere Island and which frequently are foster parents for Shining cuckoos.

Don says today that he hardly expected to be granted permission for the experiment to proceed. Tampering with the eggs of one of the world's rarest birds, moving them into the nests of strangers, destroying robins' nests in the hope that they would start again — this was a responsibility not to be taken lightly. Still there seemed to be no other way. Permission was granted and in the season of 1980–81 the cross-fostering programme began.

At this time we were also fortunate to be given permission to come back with our television cameras to film the historic events for a second black robin documentary.

From the beginning this expedition was different from the first for us. There wasn't the high adventure of climbing around cliffs, but there was the unique opportunity of getting to know the black robins themselves, now that they had settled into their new home on Mangere Island. As one of our team said:

When you go to an island to look for a rare and endangered bird, you expect to have to search for it — that's part of the fun, part of what you expect — to have to work for it. But you're not in the bush five minutes, and the robins find you! *And the first time you're aware of them, they're liable to be about half a metre from your face, looking you boldly in the eye with their bright beady eyes. They're so tiny, and so helpless really. But they break right into that personal distance barrier, safety zone, that people have. They're friendlier than friendly. . . .*

As the cameraman began trying to film them in the dim light of the forest, and the sound man tried to catch their song amongst the rustling of the trees, we came to know the birds as individuals. One had the habit of getting up very early in the morning, and singing until late into the night. Each of the robins had its own personality.

Everyone on the island was waiting to see when the birds would begin nesting. Once again there were only two females. One of these was Old Blue from Little Mangere. At last brief courtship displays were observed and filmed. Then Old Blue was seen collecting ribbonwood bark and moss to line her nest. Before long her nest was found, with two eggs in it. By this time the other female was beginning to nest too. The cross-fostering programme was about to begin.

Don Merton and his assistant Dave Crouchley, a Wildlife trainee, had already found many of the warbler nests on the island, and now picked the one which would be best for Old Blue's eggs. Don left the eggs with their own mother to be incubated for the first vital days. Then, on a fine still day, be began the tricky job of moving them over. He lifted the eggs out with a little plastic scoop, and transferred them to a small aluminium container, padded with cottonwool. He carried this over to the new nest inside his woollen shirt, moving slowly and carefully. When the warblers were away from their

Chatham Island warbler nest and 'foster' eggs. Photo Rod Morris

nest feeding, their own eggs were taken out, to be moved to another warbler nest, and one black robin egg together with an artificial egg was placed carefully inside.

Everyone watched anxiously to see what would happen when the warblers came back. Would they begin brooding the alien eggs as their own? They did — and on schedule one of the eggs hatched. (The second egg had turned out to be infertile.) The foster parents were soon feeding the black robin chick as their own. And the other female had now laid her eggs, so they were also transferred to warbler nests. Everyone was jubilant.

Our television crew naturally didn't want to disturb the birds by going too close to the foster nests. However we did get an idea of what was happening by filming at another nest where a warbler mother was raising her own chick. We strengthened the suspended woven nest with florist's wire and cut a window in the back, covered with glass, so that the scene inside became visible and filmable. The cameraman came to know when to begin the camera rolling to get the film we wanted. The chicks could sense their mother coming long before she arrived, and showed signs of excitement. Then she would arrive at the nest entrance with a green caterpillar or juicy spider for the nestlings which they greedily gobbled down. It was possible to imagine similar scenes in the nests holding the black robin chicks.

But no one could imagine everything that was going on there. It was a great shock when, one day, the warbler foster parents lost interest in the nest containing Old Blue's chick. When Don Merton looked inside, he found the chick dead, just ten days after it had hatched. The nest was cut open to see why this had happened. It had been badly fouled, which may have been one cause of death. But Don thought that the main cause was probably starvation. The warblers weren't bringing the robin chicks enough of the foods they needed to survive. Though willing, warbler foster parents could not safely raise black robin chicks past about ten days.

What was to be done now? The other female's chick, hatched a few days after Old Blue's, had been in a warbler's nest for a week and would probably die if left there much longer. Old Blue had just laid a second clutch of eggs, and the other female looked as if she was getting ready to nest again too. What was going to happen to the extra eggs which were being produced?

There seemed to be only one solution. The chicks would have to be "back-fostered" to black robins after a few days in warbler nests — although to give them all a fair chance of survival would require some complicated juggling.

While Old Blue was off feeding, her second clutch of eggs was removed to warbler nests. The other female robin's chick was taken from the warbler nest where it had been for a week and put in Old Blue's nest. Everyone watched anxiously. Would Old Blue accept a chick in place of the two eggs she had left when she went out? She did, and was soon hunting around busily for food for the chick.

By further juggling of eggs and chicks in this way, a total of three young robins was raised to independence that season — more than for many years. Of course, the juggling act was full of strain for the Wildlife people. Our cameraman made a note in his journal at that time:

Poor Don — what a worry. Having the chances of survival of a species resting on your next decision. Of course, everything he does is a calculated risk — there is no one or nothing to say, "yes, that was right" or "no, that was wrong."

However the decisions were right, and soon people were excited by the success of the experiments. Once again new ground had been broken in New Zealand in an effort to save an endangered species. As a columnist in a major newspaper wrote the following year:

It is perhaps too much to hope for, but New Zealanders should accord its Wildlife Service, and particularly officer Don Merton, the sort of adulation and support usually given to the country's sporting heroes.

Now there were eight black robins.

It was obvious that warblers were not a satisfactory long-term solution to the black robin problem. Another foster parent had to be found that could raise the robin chicks right through to independence.

Already, during the 1980–81 season, while we were filming our documentary about cross-fostering on Mangere Island, Don Merton was beginning to think about the next move. He had decided to try the Chatham Island tomtit as the new foster parent. This bird no longer existed on Mangere, but was flourishing on a larger island of the Chathams group, known as South East — a good hour's boat trip away. Would the robin eggs or very young chicks tolerate such a trip? Would the tomtits accept them?

The director of our programme remembers seeing Don preparing for the experiments he would begin next season:

We were filming warblers when we saw Don walk past with a box, which he seemed to be carrying around Mangere Island. About half an hour later he walked back, and then he walked past again about an hour after that. Finally we asked him what he was doing and he opened the box for us. Inside was a heated tin of corned beef.

There was a cup on top of it lined as a soft nest. Sitting in the little nest was a tiny warbler chick, quite naked, being swung around the island.

Don was simulating a trip from Mangere to South East Island for the young chick. At that time he was formulating plans to take the robins to South East, and this showed that he was, if not a perfectionist, a man who really tried to minimise the risks as much as he could — and he certainly had enough risks in the egg-juggling. He had no fancy electronic incubator out there to keep these things warm, so he had to heat this can of corned beef which he figured would hold its warmth for a reasonable time.

The next season the news came that Don had taken the first egg across to South East. He had to go by a fisherman's "fizz boat" and was worried by the effects of the extreme vibration of the small craft on the egg. The egg did get there safely, but now the question was whether a tomtit would accept the egg and incubate it.

Some days later, back on Mangere, Don heard on the radio-telephone from South East that the egg had hatched under the tomtit and the chick was doing well. In time it was established that tomtits could do what the warblers could not — raise the young robins to independence.

Don saw South East as a far more promising island for the robins than Mangere. It had a much larger area of forest, showing vigorous regeneration since removal of the sheep in 1961. The robins and tomtits would share this environment well, as they had in historic times, exploiting different levels in the forest. (Tomtits often catch flying insects in the air and search for grubs in the trees, while robins spend most of their time feeding on insects on the ground.)

In the following season, a number of black robin eggs and chicks were taken to South East, but had to be returned to Mangere once independent. Then as the breeding population began to increase, permission was granted to establish black robins on South East Island, and in 1983 the first robin pairs were taken from Mangere to South East to found a second population.

Don did find there were some unexpected complications. Black robins raised by tomtits seemed very reluctant to breed with black robins. Growing up with tomtit parents, the young robins had come to think they were tomtits — a process known as "mal-imprinting". However Don got over this by taking the mal-imprinted black robins to Mangere, where there were no tomtits. As there were only black robins to breed with there, the young birds soon resolved their problem. Unable to continue to take all the young robins back to the small Mangere forest, Don re-introduced a "back-fostering" programme with robin parents and tomtit-raised chicks — although the timing was not nearly as critical as it had been with the warblers. He found that if the young robins were taken out of the tomtit nests and returned to a robin nest a few days before they fledged (when they were beginning to notice what kind of bird was feeding them) they reached maturity knowing they were black robins. In this way, the adult black robins were still induced to lay more clutches and tomtits took care of the additional eggs. Broods of similar age were then united and returned to the few robin pairs for fledging — and the population grew. In the more expansive environment of South East, the young robins also began breeding when they were a year old, rather than two years old as they had on the other islands, so everything was happening more quickly.

Over the next three seasons, the number of black robins soared, reaching as high as thirty-eight birds — with the larger number on South East although there was still a growing colony on Mangere.

In the 1985–1986 season, it was decided that a film crew should go and see the black robins in their new home, and collect film for a third documentary about them.

It was exciting to see them in the new environment. Our cameraman remembers:

Throughout ten years of intermittently filming the black robin I'd always had to film the birds in the forests, so they were up against the forest canopy — black against green. But about two days before I had to leave South East I came out of the forest and there was one of the chicks sitting out in the sun! For the first time I was able to film black robin against clear blue sky instead of in horrible dim light. It was so unusual and it only happened on this one occasion. In the sun against the blue sky

Chatham Island tomtit foster parent feeding black robin fledgling. Photo Dave Crouchley

background it was just so different! I went back to the hut that night on top of the world.

It was exciting, too, just to see more black robins about. And there were many interesting new developments to Don's techniques in protecting the birds — for example he now used nest-boxes with their entrances protected by large-mesh screens to prevent intruders such as seabirds or starlings from disturbing the nests.

Don told us that he planned to carry on the cross-fostering programme for one more season, before leaving the robins to breed on their own. After that he will still keep a watchful eye on them. But he is adamant that, barring a cataclysm, the black robin has made it. He said:

In a way, it would be nice just to leave the robins alone. They've been through enough really. They've been hounded and manipulated and so on for a long time, and they've responded well to it — they've been a wonderful bird to work with. It's been as if they wanted to co-operate and knew the future of their species depended on it.

But Don still has plans for helping the black robin. He wants to establish a third black robin colony on nearby Pitt Island, a rat-free island of 6000 hectares and gentle terrain. A large healthy forest remains at the southern end of the long island, while the northern end is occupied by a small farming community. This consists of ten families of "Pitt Islanders" most of whom are descended from the original settlers of about 1840, making Pitt one of the oldest farming communities in New Zealand. They have warmed over the years to the black robin rescue mission and to the men of the Wildlife Service undertaking it. They have provided vital boat transport, and helped with free food and accommodation, and have now offered land and help with fencing for the new black robin colony on their island. As Don Merton says, "Without their help the Black Robin project could never have taken place — its success is a tribute to their goodwill." Perhaps they identify somewhat with the robin, being a tiny island community themselves, with a pure blood-line of ancestry. The black robin has become a symbol for them.

The robins have certainly come a long way since those first risky transfers down the cliff-face of Little Mangere ten years ago. The rescue team would have felt even more desperate then had they known what was only revealed later — that only Old Blue would prove to be an effective breeding female. So the effective breeding population of the black robin from 1979 to 1983 was in fact just one pair! Thus all fifty robins alive in 1987 are descended from Old Blue.

The significance of Old Blue's survival for fourteen years and her production to the end have only now become apparent. No robin since has lived anywhere near that age — most live less than half. Had she not survived for such an amazingly long time the black robin would certainly be extinct now. Old Blue saved the species.

Chatham Islands black robin, 'Old Blue'. Photo Don Merton

Chapter Eight

Yellow-eyed Penguin

Sea Bird of the Land

ONE OF THE FIRST WILD SOUTH documentaries to feature penguins was about wildlife on the Snares Islands, a hundred kilometres south-west of Stewart Island. The main character in the film was a striking bird known as the Snares crested penguin because it lives nowhere else in the world. Our film showed penguins marching single-file through fern and bush, making nests under the spreading green umbrellas of punui leaves, and climbing among the twisted trunks and branches of huge *Olearia* trees, almost as if they were using playground equipment.

It was an image very different from the conventional one of regimented penguins on the ice. But the conventional image is misleading. Of the seventeen species of penguin in the world, only two are true Antarctic species — the well known adelie penguin and the mysterious and giant emperors, standing over a metre high. Other penguins live on islands and coastal margins all around the Southern Hemisphere, and one (the Galapagos penguin) even occupies islands on the Equator.

Mainland New Zealand enjoys the company of nine penguin species, more varieties than any other country. We have been called the "penguin capital of the world".

One of the most interesting is the yellow-eyed penguin, known to the Maori as hoiho, probably after one of the distinctive calls it makes. Its English name comes from its eerie yellow eyes, set in a band of yellow which circles its head like a coronet. The yellow-eyed penguin has the dubious distinction of being perhaps the rarest penguin in the world. Altogether there may only be 5000–7000, all found in the coastal waters of Southern New Zealand and its outlying sub-antarctic islands. Our mainland beaches may support about 1000, and one of its last important breeding areas is the Otago Peninsula — within thirty kilometres of the Natural History Unit office.

We had been to many remote islands and corners of New Zealand to make *Wild South* films before we filmed this one, virtually on our doorstep.

The first idea was just to make a straight documentary, showing yellow-eyed penguins nesting and raising their chicks throughout a season. But then a much more exciting project began taking shape. As research was being done for the programme, we began to realise that it might be possible to tell the story of a particular pair of birds — a story which had been recorded in all its detail, forty years before. Like a novel of penguin life, it told of a devoted penguin couple, who expressed their "affection" in all sorts of demonstrative ways. They had a pair of chicks when the male was already very old, went through a gruelling period of raising those chicks in extremely difficult conditions, felt the stresses and strains of parenthood affecting their relationship with each other — but remained a "devoted" couple in spite of everything. Their movements, gestures and utterances had been recorded almost as fully as if they had been able to talk about their lives.

Of course, we could not hope to get to know any penguins as well as this during the short time we had to make a television programme. But we could share the understanding shown in the writings of a most remarkable man.

Lancelot Eric Richdale had devoted a large part of his life to studying the yellow-eyed penguins on the Otago Peninsula, and his work resulted in one of the most elaborate studies of bird behaviour ever made. The story of how he came to know the penguins was fascinating in itself. His life work began almost accidentally. After beginning his career as a teacher in the North Island, he became agricultural adviser to the Otago Education Board. (Many children of those days remember him fondly as the "Nature Study Man" who used to take them out of stuffy classrooms into the outdoor world.) Initially his interest was in botany. It was through a chance happening that his interest turned to sea-birds. One day, in 1935, on a botanical expedition, he was told by a farmer, annoyed that a previous visitor had left a gate open, to leave the land on which he was searching for plants. Richdale wondered what to do with the rest of his day, and recalled the enthusiastic remarks of some children he'd been teaching: "I remembered an invitation I had from some schoolchildren to go and look at penguins."

He travelled down to the Peninsula coast, and soon became absorbed watching these curious birds. Though they were obviously designed primarily for diving swiftly through the water, he marvelled at the agility with which they crossed rough, rocky beaches, and climbed steep coastal slopes. They seemed to be sociable, and gathered together on the beaches. But when he searched for their nests, they were found in all sorts of odd spots, scattered over the landscape. They seemed to like to nest secretively. Most of all, Richdale was fascinated by the strange rituals and gestures which they made to each other — standing on tip-toe, throwing their heads back, holding their flippers forward, calling to the sky. They were obviously communicating in ways Richdale could not understand. He wanted to find out the meaning of their posturing and signalling.

Richdale began searching the coast to discover penguin families and learn more of their private lives. Gradually he came to know them as individual characters. As he wrote later:

What fragmentary knowledge I possess of penguins and their ways has been acquired by spending many, many hours among them. Really to gain just a little understanding of birds it is necessary almost to live with them. This I have had to do with the penguins. Over a period of eleven years something like 1000 visits, involving travelling 40,000 miles by car, have been made to different colonies.

He went out at all hours and in all seasons, bumping his car over the thirty kilometres

Yellow-eyed penguins ashore on winter's evening. Photo Rod Morris

of unsurfaced road, over and over again. Often he stayed in the breeding areas for unbroken periods of several days and nights, sleeping out amongst the penguins. His athletic figure, sometimes grotesquely clad in longjohns for freedom and with a World War I airman's helmet for protection against the blustering winds, was seen climbing around rocks and cliffs to get to the birds.

His wife often went with him, and helped him handle the large, powerful birds to find out how they gained and lost weight at different stages of their lives.

It was frequently the lot of my wife, constant companion of the majority of my excursions, to grapple with irate penguins with snapping mandibles, scratching claws, and, worst of all, whirring flippers, while I attended to other matters. . . . The method of weighing was to place the bird in a sugar-bag and then use a spring balance accurate to a quarter of a pound.

However the main object was not to understand the physical characteristics of the penguins, but their behaviour and the pattern of their lives.

To make sense of what he saw, Richdale banded the birds — which was no easy job in the 1930s, when attempts to study sea-birds by tagging them with rings on their legs were being pioneered. Richdale made the rings himself, designing them so that they didn't interfere with the movement of the birds. He cut the rings out of sheet aluminium and stamped them by hand with inscription and number, marked clearly enough to be read at a distance with binoculars or telescope. Each bird was given a letter of the alphabet to show which breeding area it came from, and its own identification number. The birds were referred to in Richdale's writings by such names as X15 and B77, rather like secret service agents. As his studies continued, he wearied of the mechanical work of ring-making: "Making one's own becomes very tiresome, and I really am very sick of it now," he wrote after some years. But only through reliable identification and long observation was Richdale able to build up life-histories of the penguins in a way which had never been done before.

This was his great achievement. As he wrote with some pride:

I can truthfully say that I know *my penguins, and from this knowledge one feature of bird behaviour, in particular, has been forcibly brought home to me. It is the strong individual variation in behaviour . . .*

He had found that the birds were as different from each other as people are.

His major interest was in the sexual and family relationships of the penguins, and in 1947, he recorded a major breakthrough in this understanding. Richdale had discovered that while many penguins had long-lasting "marriages" about eighteen per cent were "divorced" and re-mated. As the Australian magazine *Wildlife* announced at the head of one of Richdale's articles that year:

The author tells for the first time of the existence and extent of relationships equivalent to marriage and divorce in a bird community.

He described the occasion on which he made this discovery, showing how closely he had come to follow the lives of particular birds:

I once found a certain female penguin, by number 73, associating with a male penguin, 72, whose wife 65 was at sea. I happened to arrive at the nest just as 65 was coming home.

It was almost dark as I slipped behind a tree trunk to watch. Soon I heard flippers beating mercilessly on another penguin's back. Female 73 took her thrashing without retaliation, and was ejected from the nest by the irate 65. Such is the law in the penguin world.

The two penguins, 73 and 72, seemed to forget their illicit relationship, and went back to living faithfully with their usual partners for the next two years, both raising chicks. However the female 73 had not forgotten her attraction to 65's "husband". At the end of the second season, just after the chicks had left the nests, 65 disappeared, probably meeting her death in some way. The following year, 73 mated with 65's "husband", and they remained together until 73 lost her life in a rabbit trap.

Richdale believed that:

The discovery of the affinity of 73 for 72 was one of the most important pieces of research I have ever made on penguins. It has contributed much to the study of bird behaviour. . . . It was only because I had known the birds personally for some years that I was able to happen on that eventful evening when night was falling.

Richdale's work is full of the stories of individual birds, built up patiently over many years.

As a doctor keeps a record of his patients, so do I of the penguins. I know all about their private affairs — their various "wives" and "husbands". Some according to our standards are faithful and have remained mated to the same partner for seven consecutive seasons. Then again, others have had several mates. One pair even "remarried" after having been "divorced" and "married" to other birds for a season. There are now grandchildren "married" with families of their own. . . .

However it seemed that one story had been particularly important to Richdale — that of the birds he called Z12 and 115. It kept cropping up in his writings, a tale not of faithlessness but of long and loyal faithfulness.

Z12 was the bird Richdale studied for the longest time. As far as he could establish Z12 was the oldest bird on the peninsula at that time. Z12 was already mated when Richdale met him, so he must have been at least three years old then. He was observed for ten years and must have been at least thirteen when he died — perhaps older. Richdale speculated that he may have even been twenty years old. The most interesting thing about Z12 was the depth of feeling he showed towards his "wife" 115. Richdale wrote:

As I watched Z12 and his family day after day I could not help noticing that Z12 behaved towards 115 and the chicks in a way that was closely akin to affection. The visual and auditory stimuli of the family on his behaviour were most marked.

It seemed that the best focus for the *Wild South* documentary was the story of these birds during the season which Richdale described most fully. Of course, they had died years before. Would it be possible to film penguin couples as if they were Z12 and 115, and illustrate some of the story which Richdale had described?

Following page Papanui beach, Otago Peninsula. Photo Rod Morris

We decided to show the observer as well as the observed — the figure of a man patiently watching the birds, and recording their story. Richdale had died not long before we came to make our programme. To show a figure representing him in this way would be a tribute to his remarkable work.

There were new problems for the *Wild South* in the human side of this story — finding someone to play the part of Richdale, with clothes, car and equipment which were characteristic of the 1930s and '40s when he did his major research. However these were technical problems which were fairly easily overcome.

The real challenge was in finding penguins who would behave in the ways Richdale had described Z12 and 115 behaving, in order to re-create the story of his favourite birds.

The most important thing at the beginning was to establish the strength of the pair bond, and the director decided that the best way to do this was to show a pair of birds moulting in autumn. Moulting is an extremely arduous activity for penguins. It comes at the end of the breeding season, when they are usually thin and weary. They have to spend 3½ weeks shedding their old coats for the new, before the cold winter months, and during this time the penguins cannot go to sea to feed. With typical thoroughness, Richdale had found, by weighing the birds, that they lost half their body weight while they waited for their new plumage to emerge. He had also found that a strongly-mated couple usually moulted together, and stayed together until the moulting process was completed. Even if one was ready to go to sea for food before the other, it would wait patiently until its mate was ready to follow. This seemed to be a way of confirming the pair bond.

We were lucky to find a pair who exactly illustrated this behaviour. One bird stood on a wind-swept coastal cliff, shedding its old coat in rags and patches — a tatty and forlorn sight. Its partner, neatly clad in shiny new feathers, waited patiently just below it, buffeted by the cold winds and suffering from hunger. The cameraman filmed our Richdale-figure watching the birds through a long telescope. The scene graphically established the stoicism of the yellow-eyed penguins, and of the man who had chosen to study their lives.

The next step was to give an impression of Z12 and 115 relaxing at sea during the winter months, which Richdale called their "holiday" time. Although the birds keep coming ashore from time to time, their most important winter activity is feeding at sea, getting fat and fit for the coming breeding season. The director decided that the scene we wanted was of Richdale watching the penguins gracefully riding the wild waves as they came in for a spell on land. However we had some adventures of our own when it came to filming the penguins in the surf.

To film them at close quarters without frightening them, we built a wall of rocks at the edge of the tide, and covered it with hessian to make a hide. On one occasion a wave surged up to the hide, and spilled the round boulders everywhere — which terrified the cameraman as well as the penguins! We had to accept, as Richdale had, that the penguins' lives at sea must remain largely outside our knowledge.

Moulting yellow-eyed penguin. Photo Rod Morris

Filming began in earnest in early spring, at the first signs of the breeding season. We began by looking for a nest site like the one Richdale had described for Z12 and 115:

[They] lived in dense bush. Among the big trees were rimu, matai, miro, kamahi and broadleaf. Several smaller trees were the kowhai, beautiful in the spring with its pretty yellow flowers; several kinds of maples, lacebark, lancewood and ngaio. Climbing over the trees were lawyer and supple-jack. The latter was always a mass of attractive red berries in late winter. . . .

This was a traditional type of nesting site for yellow-eyed penguins, and the kind of environment in which they had evolved. The Peninsula coast had once been covered with ancient, often dense forest in which the yellow-eyed penguins had developed their behaviour as birds of land and sea. The cool damp forests had enabled them to spend much time ashore in spite of the thick layer of fat they needed under their skins to keep them warm in the chilling cold of the southern seas. However, by Richdale's time, most of this forest had been cleared and burned. By the time we came to make our film, there remained even fewer patches of scrub and bush.

After much searching we found a well-used nest site under an old ngaio tree. This was the closest we could get to a traditional environment. Fortunately it was also in a place where we were unlikely to be bothered by people — another new problem for a film about rare birds. Even the remote corners of the Otago Peninsula are frequently visited by residents and tourists, and we were very conscious that a day's filming could be wrecked by a well-meaning person coming to have a chat.

We constructed an unusually strong hide. It was very clear from Richdale's writings that the secretive yellow-eyed penguin would be ill-at-ease if it had to conduct its family life in the presence of other penguins, much less humans. The coast is sometimes pounded by strong winds even in summer, and we did not want the hide to flap and disturb the penguins, making them aware of our presence during the long months of filming. So we lugged up heavy iron spikes and marine plywood and built a sturdy, immovable hide, from which we could watch and film even in gales, without alarming the birds.

In early September, we began waiting for the pair of birds to arrive — hoping that they would turn out to be suitable stand-ins for Z12 and 115.

The first one to be seen was the male who waddled along, picked up some grass and sticks in its beak, and threw them on the heap of sticks left from the year before. Then he sat down and had a rest. His efforts at nest-building seemed rather half-hearted, but we knew from Richdale's writings that his main reason for being there was to wait for the female to arrive. The male yellow-eyed penguin is ready to mate before the female.

Then the plump female arrived, and was greeted by her mate with signs of "delight". It was just like a description of Z12 and 115:

[He] immediately stood up on his toes, stretched out his flippers in front of him like stiff cards, pushed his head straight up to the sky, opened his mouth, and poured forth his beautiful semi-musical song . . .

It seemed as if we had chosen a good couple for our story. However they weren't yet ready to play out the drama of their breeding and nesting season. The female didn't stay long, but left the nest-site to make her way back to the sea. Over the next two weeks, each time the cameraman went back, the male was still alone at the nest, getting thinner and thinner. Sometimes the female visited him briefly, but would soon leave again for the sea.

The director began to wonder if perhaps her affections were being stolen by some other male, and all our efforts at this nest site were going to be wasted. We climbed carefully down to the beach to see what was happening there. There were many birds loitering around on the sand, probably adolescents, divorced birds, widows, widowers, or just loners. (Richdale had estimated that up to 30% of the adult population were unmated each season.) Some of the male birds made advances to our female as she waddled across the sand. It was easy to recognise one gesture which Richdale had called the "Salute" and described in detail:

A bird apparently interested in a female will start from six to fifteen feet away with his back to her and, according to the human observer, will seem to be quite indifferent to her presence. He must, however, be fully conscious of her, for suddenly he turns around and, with neck arched, with beak nearly touching the ground, and with flippers pushed out stiffly in front of him, he rapidly walks up to her and past her with quaint little steps, stops with his back to her, and thrusts his beak straight up to the sky, with his neck fully stretched, and with his flippers still thrust out in front. Reaching to his full height he maintains this position for about five seconds before slowly lowering and turning his head, almost simultaneously looking over one shoulder as if to gauge the effect.

This elaborate gesture was almost like a multi-flourished courtly bow. To our relief, our female was oblivious to such attentions. If she wasn't hurrying out to sea for food, she was hurrying back to the nest to be greeted enthusiastically by her mate.

But then there was another worry. One day, as the cameraman crept back to the hide at the nest-site, he found that neither bird was there. We hunted about, and discovered that they had shifted to a site in a paddock, a little further inland. For a while we wondered if our presence had scared them away. Then a dead hare, partly eaten by a ferret, was found by the old nest site. It seemed more likely that this was what had frightened them. Predators are one of the great dangers facing the yellow-eyed penguin during the nesting season. The next night we set a trap, which caught the ferret. Then, by placing a large rock in the middle of our couple's new nest (while they were both away for a short time) we persuaded them to go back to the old ngaio-tree site. Next morning, the male was waiting there again.

It wasn't long after this that we could see that the preliminaries to the breeding season were over. We did not attempt to film the act of mating, as Richdale had not seen this in all his years of observation. But it was obvious that it had taken place. The female's behaviour changed abruptly. Suddenly she was spending all her time at the nest, while the male was spending most of his time at sea fattening up after his long fast.

After a few days, the female laid one egg, much to the excitement of the male when he came back and saw it. Four days later, she laid another, and the two birds began to take turns at sitting on the nest to keep the eggs warm.

For six weeks, the birds came and went in a fairly relaxed way, sometimes staying away for two or three days at a time before coming back to take over the incubation of the eggs. Our crew came and went rather intermittently, too. Then one day the cameraman came back to find that the eggs had just hatched. The new nestlings were tiny. Richdale described them as "two helpless bits of life covered in dark-coloured down and weighing just three ounces."

Now the difficult part of the season was beginning. Three months of very hard work lay ahead for our pair, as they took turns at going out to sea every day to bring back food for the chicks.

As the cameraman watched and filmed, he became fascinated with the birds' greeting behaviour each time they met. Richdale had made an extensive catalogue of penguin "language, both vocal and physical" and coined quaint descriptive terms for the different signals: "The Sheepish Look, the Throb, the Shake, the Gawky Look, the Open Yell, the Ecstatic Arms Act, the Bow, the Welcome, the Mutual Preen, the Kiss Preen, the Half Trumpet, and the Full Trumpet."

He also gave detailed descriptions of the ways the signals were used, such as this one of Z12 returning to the nest:

As the male appears in sight, the female usually gives a quick look straight at her partner and breaks into an "open-yell", whereupon the male walks up to her quickly. Close beside her he performs a "half-trumpet". Together they then give several "half trumpets", which end in the adoption of the "sheepish look". Resuming an erect posture and facing each other, both birds indulge in the full "welcome". This is repeated a number of times before gradually subsiding into "half trumpets", "throbs", and "sheepish looks". The male then looks behind the female, which walks away from the nest. He thereupon straddles the chicks, runs his beak over them, and then sits down on them. Meanwhile the female has moved away a metre or two for preening before finally lying down for a sleep. As this is going on, the male is poking the chicks to make them interested in food.

It was challenging to try to identify these signals and film such scenes. They showed vividly the feelings the penguins had for each other, and the "emotional support" they gave each other during the hard work of raising their chicks. Of course we could not understand what was going on as well as Richdale had, but still felt involved in their lives.

The chicks gained about a kilogram of weight a week, and were soon becoming as plump as footballs. After four weeks, they were too big to be straddled by either parent, and the adult birds now took turns at standing guard over them.

At the end of six weeks, near Christmas time, the young birds were barely a head shorter than their parents, and well able to look after themselves. (When a frisky lamb approached one, the young penguin nipped it sharply and scared it away.) But there was little sign of feathers appearing through their down, so it was still a long time before they would be able to go to sea to catch their own food.

Yellow-eyed penguins at sunset. Photo Rod Morris

Now that they were so large, it was impossible for one parent to carry back enough food to satisfy the appetite of both chicks. Both father and mother began going out to sea each day to bring back food, leaving the chicks to fend for themselves. This was exhausting work for the adult birds. At sea, they were in their element, as graceful and free-moving as any bird in the air. But the trek back to the nest, when they were swollen with food, might take an hour or two. They often stopped to pant and rest in the afternoon sun. The track up the coastal cliff was as full of obstacles as one Richdale described in detail:

From the landing ground just off the beach the birds travel 72 yards up a 20-degree slope which ends in a sharp rise before bringing them onto a ridge. Another 55 yards on a comparable slope ends in a sharp rise of 15 feet to a plateau 22 yards wide. For the next 66 yards, the birds traverse a steep rough cliff with an incline of approximately 60 degrees. At the top of the steep part is a gentle slope of 70 yards culminating in the highest point of all, some 300 feet above sea level. A further 130 yards across the top brings the birds to a down grade of 45 yards to a hollow which contains the nest. Climbing to the top must be an exceptionally difficult task, especially for the parents when loaded with two or more pounds of food for the chicks.

After two or three weeks of these daily journeys, both parents were looking thin and exhausted. When they met again at the nest site, they often seemed to have little energy for the displays of affection which had been so much part of their lives earlier. They had to hurry to feed their large, hungry, raucous chicks. Then they might just want to rest. As Richdale wrote: "the adults are seemingly unable to take much notice of each other, and love-habits between them are less in evidence."

However there were some scenes which showed that they still felt the same bond — almost like this one Richdale described, with Z12 and 115:

On 17 January the female did not come home until 10.50 p.m. unusually late indeed. All the intensive love-habits were used that night and were kept up for a considerable time. Both birds employed the "full trumpet" frequently; the whole pandemonium was interspersed with the pleading calls of the chicks. The latter, of course, were usually responsible for the break-down of the home-coming ceremonies of the parents.

When the chicks were ten weeks old, they were as tall as their parents, and much fatter and stronger-looking. Yet their thin, weary parents still had several weeks of feeding them ahead. The hardest part of the season was still to come.

It was just at this point that we stopped our film.

Of course we would normally have followed the season through to the end, showing the chicks shedding their soiled down for bright new feathers and leaving the nest for the sea. But in this film we were trying to re-create the lives of Z12 and 115, and we could follow them no further. For in that season, the usual pattern changed.

Richdale described the subsequent events in detail in his writings.

On the night of the 25th January, he was concerned to see that Z12 and 115 seemed to have had something of a rift. After returning first, and feeding the chicks, 115 hid in

Yellow-eyed penguin chicks. Photo Rod Morris

some long grass. When Z12 arrived back, he called appealingly to his mate, but she made no reply. Richdale watched until midnight, but she remained hidden.

When Richdale arrived at 8 a.m. next morning, both birds had gone out to sea as usual. Although a bad storm was brewing up, he waited faithfully and watched for their return. He was rewarded by witnessing their warm reconciliation:

At 5.40 p.m. *on January 26, during heavy rain, 115 returned, fed the chicks, and took up her position as she had the night before. Z12 returned at 7.05* p.m. *and after a careful look around gave a "full trumpet". This time the hidden female replied. The effect on the male was immediate. He gave a quick look in the direction of the call, stood up on his toes, and uttered one of the most vigorous "full-trumpets" I have ever heard. By 7.13* p.m. *the chicks were fed, and the male hurried along to the female; then intensive love-habits were performed. All night they stayed together, leaving the chicks some distance away unguarded. Next morning both parents entered a very rough sea. From this expedition Z12 never returned.*

The disappearance of the old penguin was a shock to the man who had watched him for so long. Day after day, Richdale scanned the beach in the hope that Z12 would be amongst the incoming penguins. But Z12 had been claimed by the sea. Richdale felt the loss of "the old man of the Peninsula" sharply.

When he went back to see 115 and her hungry pair of chicks, he was concerned to see that she was disturbed and confused by the disappearance of her mate. Although the chicks were pleading loudly for food, she seemed incapable of continuing her parental duties. She came and went from the nest most irregularly for several days. Four days after Z12 had disappeared, she stayed away for two days, the first time the chicks had ever been left alone at night. On a subsequent morning, she set out early, as if to go to the sea for food, but stopped half-way to the sea, and did not move for more than twenty-four hours. For ten days, the chicks received very little food. Then 115's confusion passed, and she began again to try to feed the chicks, as devotedly as before.

It was soon apparent though that without her mate she had little hope of bringing back enough food to satisfy the two chicks, who were now larger than herself. Richdale saw that one of the chicks was becoming dominant, and seizing most of the food which the weary mother brought back. He found himself calling the chicks "Fat" and "Skin" — and he could see that day by day "Skin" was becoming weaker. At last, the chick simply lay down and made no attempt to win his share of food. His mother did her best to encourage the skinny chick to eat, and Richdale watched in surprise when she pushed her fatter chick away and advanced excitedly to the weakling to regurgitate all the food she had. Sadly, it was not enough to restore his strength. Her task of feeding both chicks was impossible.

Finally Richdale intervened to save Z12's last chicks. Naturally he could not provide them with the food to which they were accustomed. He decided to feed "Skin" with mussels. The chick fiercely resisted the interference from the well-meaning stranger, but Richdale caught and force-fed him with the mussels. The shell-fish seemed to satisfy the young bird, who soon became visibly stronger.

Yellow-eyed penguins ashore at dusk. Photo Rod Morris

For six weeks, Richdale laboured to feed the young bird. Then, one night in the middle of March, he was relieved to find that "Skin" was strong enough to obtain his share of the food from his mother again — in fact he could keep "Fat" back while he received mouthful after mouthful. For Richdale, it was a personal triumph. The two young birds had their feathers now. The next day, "Fat" admitted defeat, and took to the sea for his first swim, beginning to catch his own food. "Skin" was not yet sufficiently strong to follow, but after two more weeks of enjoying an uncontested supply of food from his mother, he too took to the sea. Richdale had successfully assumed Z12's role, and had been rewarded in seeing the old bird's last two chicks reach independence.

We were not able to film the ending to this story, but chose to conclude with a wild summer storm, a storm in which Z12 might well have lost his life. We filmed our Richdale-figure watching the coast anxiously amid the dying turmoil of the storm, and the fate of Z12's chicks was narrated in the calm which followed.

Lance Richdale had once been called by *Time* magazine "the Dr Kinsey of the penguin world". His two major books, *Sexual Behaviour in Penguins* and *A Population Study of Penguins* had been hailed in academic circles as the standard works in their field and won him an international reputation. Yet, it was through a children's book, the only one he ever wrote, that we uncovered the story of the penguin family which had been so important to him. It was by piecing together details from *Podgy the Penguin*, his story for children, with the many references to Z12 and 115 which appeared in his scientific writings that the drama unfolded. For us it captured the essential qualities of his studies of the yellow-eyed penguin.

During the process of our research, other facets of Richdale's work were revealed. There was his practical interest in the conservation and protection of the yellow-eyed penguin.

He had been very concerned about the way so much bush was being cut down, and their nests destroyed. So he worked to set up some fenced reserves for the birds. Unfortunately his efforts were not successful in his own time. Although two reserves were set up, they were not managed effectively. More trees were cut down in the following decades, and the number of yellow-eyed penguins declined drastically. In one breeding area where Richdale had recorded 200 breeding birds, there were recently found to be less than twenty pairs, from which just three chicks survived. The former home of Z12 and 115 no longer exists as a breeding area at all.

However Richdale's work has not been in vain. As we were making our film, his torch was being taken up again. Two years earlier, a scientist, John Darby, had initiated a new era of intensive research into the birds. He was concerned to find that in many of the breeding areas of the yellow-eyed penguin — not only on the mainland but on Stewart Island and the Auckland Islands — the birds were subject to many introduced dangers, especially predation by cats and ferrets. People realise that the yellow-eyed penguin is a species at risk, and new efforts are being made to set up reserves for the birds on their mainland breeding areas and plans drafted for the re-planting of native bush around these areas.

Yellow-eyed penguins preening after coming ashore. Photo Dean Schneider

John Darby said in an address on the yellow-eyed penguin to the executive of the Forest and Bird Society:

We have to report that by 1985 we had made almost no concessions to this species. It survives on the mainland not by our grace but by its sheer tenacity. There is no room for complacency for the future survival of this species.

We have to remind ourselves that Richdale, in writing of the natural history of the little blue penguin in 1942, stated that as a nesting bird it outnumbered all others on the Otago Peninsula, and that there were more than a thousand nests to be found. Forty-five years later, there remain just twenty-three nests of the little blue penguin on the Peninsula. We cannot continue with a blind belief in the tenacity of the yellow-eyed for if we do nothing I believe that it will also follow the fate of the little blue.

As this quotation shows, although one of Richdale's interests was the yellow-eyed penguin, he was also interested in little blue penguins, and in all the other species he could observe. During his years of work on the peninsula, he made notes on six other species of penguins — Fiordland crested, erect-crested, rockhopper, royal, white-flippered, little blue, and of course the yellow-eyed penguins. While he was observing Z12 and his family, he was also studying and taking notes on a pair of erect-crested penguins nesting nearby — the first mainland record for this sub-antarctic species.

Also his interest in sea-birds was not limited to penguins. He was fascinated by the strange pageant of sea-bird life. Although the mainland coasts had lost many of the species which had once filled the skies with clouds of millions of birds, Richdale often visited off-shore islands to see the sea-bird life which still survived there. He spent many weeks pioneering the study of petrels on Whero Island, off Patterson's Inlet. He studied Buller's mollymawk and mottled petrel on the Snares. He frequently visited the Mutton-bird Islands to see the sooty shearwaters and other petrels which flourished there. He was deeply aware of the richness of the tapestry of bird-life which had been lost to the mainland of New Zealand.

However, perhaps his most spectacular achievement in bird observation and conservation, apart from his work on yellow-eyed penguins, was back on his home ground of the Otago Peninsula.

In 1936, the year after he began his penguin studies, he was shown a royal albatross nest containing an egg at Taiaroa Head, near the entrance to Otago Harbour. As far as he knew this bird only nested on off-shore and sub-antarctic islands. Richdale photographed the egg, only to find shortly afterwards that it had been stolen. (There was no protection then, either from human or animal predators.)

Richdale took action, and gained the assistance of the Otago Branch of the Royal Society of New Zealand. When a further egg was laid in 1937, Richdale posted himself as guardian, sometimes sitting all day by the nest. The entire breeding cycle and the fledging of the chick — a process which took eleven months — was completed under his close observation. In 1938, he initiated further protection of the breeding area. Ferret trapping was begun, protective fencing was put up to keep humans out, and the harbour

Snares crested penguin in tree. Photo Rod Morris

master agreed to let the signalmen at the lighthouse act as unpaid wardens. The area eventually became an albatross sanctuary.

Because of these protective efforts, the royal albatross has established a small but permanent breeding colony at Taiaroa Head which has become a considerable tourist attraction. These giant oceanic birds are distant relatives of the penguins Richdale knew so well, but they evolved in utterly different ways. While the penguin is most at home "flying" through the water, the true home of the albatross is the sky above the sea, through which it soars tirelessly on wings spanning three metres. The albatross can remain at sea for years, but it must come ashore to breed. Because of Richdale and his vision, the Otago Peninsula has the world's only breeding colony of albatross on an inhabited mainland.

Only two weeks before Richdale died in 1983, the Minister of Tourism officially opened the "Richdale Observatory" at Taiaroa Head, where today many thousands of visitors come each year to observe the birds.

Of course, Lancelot Eric Richdale's real memorial is not the new building, but the fact that the albatrosses decided to stay.

Royal albatross on nest. Photo Rod Morris

Chapter Nine

Kokako

Cry of the Forest

IN THE HEART OF THE NORTH ISLAND stand the most remarkable forests in New Zealand — forests of kahikatea, totara, matai, miro and rimu. They are the most primeval forests in New Zealand, and perhaps the finest podocarp forests left on earth. The towering, living columns of wood rise with dizzying straightness to crowns which stand 30 to 60 metres above the green carpet of smaller trees. And from those lofty platforms, at sunrise and sunset, comes a call which seems quite apart from that of any living creature — beautiful yet melancholy, combining the deep, breathy richness of flute and organ pipe as though it had absorbed and now commanded the wind that tosses the forest. It is the voice of the kokako.

The kokako is almost as ancient as the forest in which it lives — being one of the three wattlebirds which come from a far distant time. The kokako has fared a little better than its two cousins. The huia is now extinct. The saddleback (the smallest of the wattlebirds) survives only on off-shore islands, while the kokako survives on the mainland, in a few forests of the North Island alone. The South Island kokako may already be extinct.

It seemed extraordinary to us, at the Natural History Unit, that so few people should have heard of, let alone heard the song of, this remarkable bird. With its soft, grey plumage, black robber-like mask across its eyes, and fleshy wattles of intense blue on either side of its burnished black beak, to some it is the most striking and beautiful bird in the entire forest.

We wanted to make a film about the kokako — something which would bring it to life in people's imaginations. But it was to become a difficult film to make.

The forests in which the kokako live are now isolated remnants of the vast expanses of trees which once covered four-fifths of New Zealand. When European settlers first arrived here, kokako were more common than tuis. They were seen in small flocks, with sometimes as many as twenty following each other in single file through the trees. As the great lowland forests were cut down for houses and ships and fences and butter-boxes, and great stretches of open land were cleared for farms and cities, over 90 percent of the forest habitat of the kokako disappeared.

The South Island kokako, which had orange wattles (sometimes almost vermilion) with a touch of blue at the base, has become so rare (because of deer and predators in the beech forests where it lived) that it is now believed to be extinct, though some recent

North Island Kokako, Puketi. Photo Rod Morris

observations could point to its survival on Stewart Island. The North Island kokako survives in the denser podocarp forests of the North, but these are only small pockets of forest today.

The forest where we decided to begin our film was Pureora, then believed to have the largest population of kokako. We soon found that, even here, the birds were hard to find and film.

The first day the film crew arrived in the forest, we stood on the ferny forest floor and looked up through the towering trees to the far-removed canopy and the patches of bright sky. It seemed almost impossible that we would ever catch sight of one of the shadowy grey birds in that gigantic landscape. (They are not large birds, about one and a half times the size of tui and not quite the size of the extinct huia.) But there on the ground it was surprising to see flashes of the same brilliant blue as the kokako's wattles. A closer look showed bright-blue mushrooms *(Entoloma hochstetteri)* growing in the moss. It seemed curious that two forms of life in the same forest should share the same amazing colour. Later we tried to find out if there were any stories about this, and learned that the Maori of the Urewera used to say that the grey birds rubbed their heads against the mushrooms, perhaps to catch some of their colour. The fungi and wattles have the same name, "werewere kokako".

As it was so difficult to see the birds in the trees, we knew that our only hope was to go back to the forest at dawn, listen to their morning songs, and then try to follow the birds by the sounds they made. We found that the dawn forest at Pureora was rich in bird song — tuis, bellbirds, kaka — but when a kokako called it was unmistakable. It was not exactly like recorded calls we'd heard — the kokako of each area have their own "dialect". However the song was so much richer and stronger than any other, we knew it could be nothing else but the bird called by early European settlers "the organ bird".

Our sound man decided to go off by himself, to follow the kokako and try to catch its sounds on tape. He knew it would be better, as usual, to work on his own and avoid any extraneous human noises. So, all day, he quietly listened and recorded every sound he heard the bird make — although he saw little of it except a grey shape moving around amongst the leaves, just enough to know where it was. After the morning recital, the bird and its mate hopped and skittered down through the branches to the understorey of the forest, where they fed and kept in touch with each other by clicking, tapping, mewing, chuckling and whistling. If they were annoyed by other birds, they sometimes flapped their short wings noisily, uttering strange screeching sounds. At the end of the day, they clambered up the giant trees again, where they gave a further haunting recital from the sun-lit tree-tops.

After following the birds around for many days, the sound man managed to collect a wonderful array of sounds on twenty-one rolls of sound-tape. Unfortunately, the cameraman was not so lucky. Whenever he caught sight of a kokako, it would dodge behind a leafy branch, which made it impossible to film. The birds all seemed determined to remain invisible, and the great size and complexity of the forest structure made it very easy for them to stay out of sight. Our first expedition brought back little film

Entoloma hochstetteri; the sky-blue toadstool. Photo Gordon Roberts

apart from remote long shots, looking up at distant views of kokako silhouetted against a bright burnt-out sky, and some film of two young fledglings who were too unsteady on their feet to get away from us quickly.

The Wildlife Service suggested we go to another forest near Rotorua, where there were a number of birds which we might be able to see better. Sure enough, when we got there, we found a ridge which looked over a small gully to another ridge where a pair of kokako lived. We set up our hide, and began watching through a 600mm telephoto lens and binoculars. Here, for the first time we found ourselves looking into the hidden world of the kokako. Instead of gazing up at them, against the sky, we could watch them against the natural background of the bush.

In all our days of wildlife filming, we had never seen a pair of birds who seemed so devoted to each other. They constantly moved around close together, clucking to each other softly, probably in case they lost visual contact in the dense foliage. It was just like the old description of huia couples, who were inseparable. Frequently one would go across to the other, and preen it around the face, chuckle to it and feed it. Then they'd be springing off again to follow each other around the trees.

Their movements were swift and surprising. They'd make incredible power dives from one tree to another, flapping their short wings frantically; crash on to a branch; race along it; then spring off again at terrific speed. Within the space of a few seconds they'd be from top to bottom of a huge tree. It was like watching squirrels rushing recklessly through the trees at breakneck speed. Their legs were long and tremendously springy, so that they seemed to bounce on coiled springs. In Maori legend these long legs are said to be a gift to the kokako from the demi-god Maui when the bird brought him water after his long battle with the sun (just as the saddleback was given a scorched back for refusing to bring that water in the same story).

We got excellent film of these two birds. Then after a few days they moved to another part of their forest territory, where we couldn't film them. We still didn't have the close-ups of their faces that we wanted, so we followed a rumour that there was a very friendly bird in Puketi forest, where kokako had recently been found. This was a kauri forest, up in Northland. No other *Wild South* film had ever involved such long journeys between shots!

When our crew got to Puketi, a Maori forester took us to the place where he said we'd see the bird. We went along rough forest roads in his four-wheel-drive vehicle. Then he stopped, got out, banged the bonnet, and said, "Come on! Come on!" After all our efforts to approach the invisible birds quietly, we could hardly believe our ears. But when we got out and crossed the track, there was the grey bird coming quietly to see us. It was like accounts of kokako in the early days, when they were very common, and used to be seen around bushmen's camps.

As we spent time watching and filming this bird, we realised that he was a lone bird who had probably lost his mate. He'd sit for hours on a branch, just watching us. He didn't exactly show curiosity — not like a bird described by an early ornithologist which dropped backwards from a branch until it hung upsidedown, and then pulled itself up

North Island brown kaka. Photo Rogan Colbourne

"like a performer on a horizontal bar" to peer at the man over the top. Our bird just seemed to want to stay quietly near us for company. The only time he dashed away from us was when we played a tape-recording of a kokako call, to get a close-up of his face in full song as he replied. Instead, he sprang off to the top of a twenty-metre tall tree, and sang back to us from there!

We couldn't get him singing in close-up, but we did get fine film of him feeding: holding leaves down with his foot and breaking them off with his beak; picking off red berries from a supplejack vine, with the glowing colour of his blue wattles against the red. We also got good close-ups of a kokako eating bag-moths — squeezing the long cocoons which dangled down from the branches to squirt out the caterpillar inside. These were the kinds of shot which we had hoped for — to fix the bird vividly in people's minds.

After this, the main thing still missing was film of nesting kokako. We knew there was no hope of getting this. Over the past hundred years, only twenty-six nests had ever been recorded (the first being found by Austrian taxidermist Andreas Reischek in 1886). Many of the nests which had been found were described as "incomplete", and others had been deserted and preyed upon. The nests found had usually been built in a fork of the main trunk of a tree, or in a dense tangle of branches, often with vines woven into them for support. Even if we had had the amazing luck to find one, it was extremely unlikely that it would have been accessible to a television camera. Yet we were sorry not to show a nest, because the kokako's nesting habits are so much a part of its story. The fact that the nests are large, and low enough in the trees to be accessible to rats or cats, is a major reason for the scarcity of kokako today.

Then we had another stroke of luck. Ten years earlier, bird-photographer Geoff Moon had filmed a nest discovered by the Maori artist Rei Hamon. He agreed to let us use this film as part of our *Wild South* programme. So we were able to show the large untidy kokako nest, with its mossy cup set in a platform of twigs, and the hungry faces of the kokako chicks with their pinkish wattles looking out from inside. Then we were able to weave in the film we'd taken earlier of two fledglings at Pureora, after they'd left the nest. Now that we had seen the agility of adult birds as they moved around the trees, we could appreciate more the coltish clumsiness of these young birds as they kept losing their balance and falling off branches. After watching the adult birds running swiftly along thin branches, the fledglings looked like inexperienced tightrope walkers.

It had taken a long time to learn the ways of kokako and collect a good range of film of kokako behaviour, but in the end with the help of a great many people over a number of years, we knew we had brought together more images of the private life of the kokako than could ever have been seen in conjunction before.

During the years we were filming the kokako, it had come to seem more and more important that we should succeed in the aims of our programme. For during these years the events of an historic story were being played out. New Zealand's conservation movement was coming into being as a powerful force, and to many people the kokako and its forest at Pureora had become key symbols for that movement, and for their feelings about the disappearing natural heritage of this land. Yet although they knew the kokako by name, its face seldom appeared in any newspaper photos — and, if it did, it looked grey and lifeless. This had strengthened our desire to make the symbol live in colour and movement on the television screen.

The story of Pureora began quietly in the early 1970s when the Wildlife Service carried out a survey of kokako habitat, and found that parts of Pureora Forest had the most flourishing populations of the birds known then. This forest was in the process of being logged by the New Zealand Forest Service. So the Wildlife reports recommended that certain areas be set aside as kokako reserves. However the voice of the Wildlife Service was not a very powerful one in government, and nothing was done.

It was just about this time, too, that the forest conservation movement was beginning in New Zealand. An organisation called the Native Forests Action Council (NFAC) organised a petition that "the logging of virgin forests (outside Westland) should be phased out". The petition gained 341,160 signatures — the largest petition ever presented to a New Zealand government at that time, showing that the conservation movement already had considerable public support. However, to bring the aims into practical effect was not easy. In battles over particular forests there was only limited success. As Guy Salmon, one of the people behind NFAC, says: "In the early years, it was a lot of slog without much victory."

Then came the battle over Pureora and the kokako.

Pureora was initially of interest to the conservation movement because it was one of the most magnificent lowland podocarp forests left in New Zealand. It had a rare mixture of the primeval giants which originated in Gondwana — kahikatea, matai, miro, rimu and tanekaha. Some of the actual trees in the forest had been growing there for over a thousand years. Beneath the ancient giants was a dense understorey of more modern flowering plants such as tawa and broadleaf. Pureora was regarded as one of the finest rainforests in the world. Living there was what had been described as a "richness of wildlife that is unique." There were kaka, North Island robins, blue duck, two species of native parakeet, the native falcon, native bat and frog. However above all there was the kokako, which was to become known as the special treasure of Pureora.

In 1977, the Native Forests Action Council became aware that the forest there was being logged. They also became aware of the Wildlife reports stating that Pureora was the most important habitat of kokako known in New Zealand. Whereas most birds could adapt to living in forests in steeper terrain, kokako were able to live only in tall lowland forests, of which Pureora was one of the finest examples. Of course, this knowledge greatly strengthened the conservationists' arguments for saving the forest. It could be argued that forests were replaceable, even if they took hundreds of years to grow, but once a bird became extinct it could never be brought back.

In April 1977 a group of NFAC supporters, led by Steve King, went to Pureora to see what was happening. They found that a large part of the forest which had been suggested as kokako reserve had already been clear-felled. Thousand-year-old totara trees, which had been no use for timber, were lying around on the ground. Now the Forest Service was just about to log the last remnant of an area which had been recommended as kokako reserve — an area which contained another stand of thousand-year-old totara trees. The only concession the loggers would make to the wishes of the conservationists and Wildlife Service people was that they would leave the totara, miro and tawa trees standing, and just cut out the rimu and kahikatea trees which were wanted for timber. However no one knew whether kokako could survive in "selectively-logged" forest of this kind.

Steve King and Guy Salmon urgently drafted a long submission, asking that the remnant of forest be made a kokako reserve. By December it was clear that Government would not accept the proposal. The logging went on. The group then dug up the logging road and planted native seedlings there, as a symbolic gesture, but the trucks drove through.

In a way it seemed impossible that a small group of conservationists should be able to stop a large government department in its tracks. However, as they spent time in the forest and became familiar with the birds as well as the trees, their determination became stronger. Guy Salmon remembers what it was like then:

I have very vivid memories of early visits to Pureora forest, standing in the areas where the trees were being felled, and hearing and seeing the birds at sunset. The intense drive we had to save that forest arose from those experiences of being in forest and seeing and hearing the birds — not only the kokako but also the kaka, which is another bird I feel strongly about. (The North Island kaka is uncommon nowadays too.) While the trees were being felled, there were great crashes reverberating through the forest, and flocks of kaka were wheeling around in the skies overhead making terrible screeching sounds and seemingly thoroughly upset and disturbed.

And I remember our first experiences of the kokako — just hearing it. I heard it for quite a long time before I actually saw one. It had the most exquisite sound. There'd be a great impenetrable greenness all round, of tawa leaves, and you couldn't work out where the sound was coming from — but the air would fill with the most beautiful, haunting song with a somewhat melancholy note at the end. Later I actually saw the birds, and they were so different from any other birds that I'd ever seen in the New Zealand forest — with their strange, almost falling motion when they were flying, and the extraordinary, almost monkey-like agility with which they ran around in the forest on those long legs. I knew they were rare and of ancient origin and I felt I was in the presence of something very different from other birds.

All round were the incredibly impressive columns of podocarp trees, and underneath the delicate lacy tawa environment, and it was so beautiful, especially in the soft early morning or evening light. That together with the sound of the kokako made one feel that one was in the presence of something quite otherworldly. One had the feeling of walking back into something enormously peaceful and still and ancient.

The feelings which the conservationists developed about Pureora led them to conceive a protest movement more dramatic than any seen before in New Zealand. At Christmas time, 1977, the logging gangs went on holiday. When they came back, fourteen pro-

North Island kokako. Photo Rod Morris

testors including five women and a boy of twelve were hidden in the tree-tops twenty metres up, with whistles to communicate with each other and provisions for a long stay — until the logging of the ancient trees was stopped.

The Forest Service tried to persuade them to leave, but without success. As one newspaper wrote:

When Forest Service officials went into the bush yesterday afternoon to ask the protesters to reconsider their position, none of them could be found. A squad of five policemen from Te Kuiti, called in to clear the protesters out of the forest, returned home without doing anything.

The dense forest could hide human beings almost as well as the kokako they were trying to help.

The loggers announced that they were determined to go on with their task of clearing the forest. To let the protesters know which trees were going to be felled, they were sprayed with dazzling orange paint. However the protesters stayed where they were and the headlines announced: "PAINT GLOWS, WHISTLES SHRILL IN FOREST WAR"; "FOREST PROTESTERS FACE DEATH AS LOGGING COMMENCES". Both sides needed strong nerves. As a newspaper report said, on January 20:

At a hastily called conference in forest headquarters yesterday morning, the district forest ranger said he nearly pulled his men out after they became 'disconcerted' at the dog whistles protesters are using to communicate with each other.

Each protester had a different whistle tone and their communication was nearly incessant, he said.

"It disturbed me because my men are pretty experienced and safety is automatic with them. If they hear a noise while felling trees they immediately react."

No one could speak directly of the fears of the hidden protesters as they wondered if their tree was to be felled next, but everyone could guess. The whole affair quickly caught the public imagination. The fate of the kokako, which the Wildlife Service had been concerned about for so long, was suddenly headline news.

The two government departments involved in the dispute, the Forest Service and Wildlife Service, were soon being questioned by the press, and making contradictory statements about whether the kokako was endangered or not. The heads of the forestry department asserted that "the kokako is widely distributed in the North Island", and in any case could survive in selectively-logged forest. Ian Crook, the wildlife officer in charge of the kokako, said:

Kokako may not yet be in danger of extinction nationally, but they have been brought into greater danger of extinction in the West Taupo area, one of their main areas, by this logging. . . . The bird's chances of survival there have been halved. . . . The kokako is now becoming a nationally endangered species and is recognised internationally as such.

Ian Crook was publicly supported by the head of his department, and also by his minister. As the headlines said: "TWO DEPARTMENTS OF STATE LOCKED OVER A NATIVE BIRD".

In the end, the loggers stopped logging, the protesters came down out of the trees, and after months of negotiations a moratorium was placed on logging in the forest for three years until thorough research could be completed into the conditions needed for the survival of kokako. Rod Hay was the scientist employed to do this work — being funded by the Forest and Bird Protection Society, and working in co-operation with the Wildlife Service.

As he wrote later:

With a pile of references, mostly old, and the sound of a snatch of Hunua Range song amongst my only previous experiences of kokako a preliminary period of getting to know them led to a strengthening of the neck muscles, a barrage of stick wounds to the shins, an appreciation of the best methods of study and an affection for the birds themselves.

Rod Hay was able to give the time to kokako that wildlife officers could give only to birds on the very brink of extinction. He selected various study areas, banded the birds in them, and followed them to find out how they fed, bred, and generally used their habitat.

After three years of research, he had established various crucial facts. One was that kokako liked to eat a huge variety of foods — beetles, cicadas, bag-moths, sixpenny-scale insects, and fruits and leaves from many different trees. The birds found their food at all levels of the forest, from the tree-tops to the ground, so they had to be able to move from one level to the other, using the network of branches as ladders, because they were such poor fliers. He found also that kokako are strongly territorial birds, and have very large territories about the size of four football fields. So quite a large area of forest was needed for each pair of birds — they would not all flock to a particular source of food if it were outside their territory. Finally, it appeared that the birds were only just finding the conditions they needed, as they had a poor breeding record — ten or fifteen pairs of nesting birds would raise only one chick in a season. This seemed to be partly because of predation and partly because, with the felling of the forest, too many birds were concentrated into too small an area. They were spending too much time defending their territory to have time to breed.

The general result of the research was to show that kokako were a species at risk, and also that they could only survive in pristine forest habitat. It was unlikely they could live in selectively-logged forest.

In 1981, the moratorium on logging at Pureora was over, and discussions began again. The government made much of the fact that they had spent $7 million in compensation to the logging companies (although conservationists argued that the payments were too high, as only 2% of this had gone to workers whose jobs had been affected). The Prime Minister, Robert Muldoon, joked that $7 million was a high price to pay for a bird; saying that "If New Zealand was offered a quantity of birds which could be found nowhere else, and the price was $7 million, I doubt whether we would buy them." For a time it seemed that the logging might be resumed. However after another round of public meetings, it was decided at last, in September 1981, that the remnant of virgin podocarp forest at

Following page *North Island Kokako with young.* *Photo N.Z. Wildlife Service*

Pureora should be protected as an ecological reserve, because this appeared to be the general wish of New Zealanders. It was a victory for the kokako, and through the kokako for New Zealand's forests and wildlife generally.

As Guy Salmon says now:

Pureora was a turning point for the forest conservation movement. Up to that time, we had fought a lot of battles which had not borne fruit — there had been no positive decision made. In the space of the period between December 1977 and August 1978, we actually completely turned around a government that was strongly committed to logging the whole forest, and they ended up by paying $7 million compensation. What that really did was to demonstrate to politicians that we had a lot of political backing — that there was a tremendous amount of support from the general public. Once we'd achieved that, all the other battles became easier to win.

In fact it turned out that from then on forests with kokako in them had a special kind of status. In 1980, a thriving population of kokako was discovered in Puketi Forest. As soon as the Wildlife Service had established that the birds were there, the Forest Service suspended logging in the areas of kokako habitat (although the forest still has no legal protection). Areas of state forest on the Mamaku Plateau were also made reserves after small populations of kokako were found there.

Even privately-owned forests could be affected. In 1983, kokako were found in a lowland forest at Oropi, which was being logged by a timber company. The Wildlife Service had always resisted moving kokako to off-shore islands, as it seemed they should be able to survive on the mainland, with human co-operation. However some birds, whose mainland forests had been destroyed, had been moved to virgin forest on Little Barrier Island where they were doing well. The Wildlife Service decided that as many as possible of the kokako at Oropi should also be moved to Little Barrier, and workers were employed to catch the birds. But some of those workers wrote vivid descriptions of what they were doing — like this one, about the catching of a kokako, by Annette Lees and Shane Wright:

He launches himself off the branch and, with lilting flight, heads towards the dummy, not seeing the delicate trap across his path. The mist-net ensnares him, mid-flight, and we spring from our shadowy hides. Pulleys bring the net down, and human hands clasp the kokako. The bird begins a heart-rending scream of terrible harshness while we struggle to free it. . . .

The male is placed in a black cloth bag. Its destiny, after being torn from its rainforest home, is a five-and-a half month wait in an eight by four cage, followed by a helicopter ride to release on Little Barrier Island. The period spent in captivity is necessary because the Government will not fund the Wildlife Service to take kokako one at a time to Little Barrier.

When events such as these were reported in the media, and the people of the Bay of Plenty learned what was going on in their region, the opposition was so great that the timber company decided not to clear the block of forest with the kokako in it.

The cry of the ancient bird had developed a strange power. And the effects of the events surrounding it went much further than just protecting the kokako itself. The forest conservation movement generally became a voice to be heard, and was successful

1000-year-old totara trees climbed by protestors to prevent logging. Photo Rod Morris

in protecting other areas of forest — sometimes because they were fine examples of particular kinds of forest, and sometimes because they were homes to other kinds of birds, or other creatures like our ancient snails and frogs. A growing number of people were coming to feel that the time had come to stop the destruction of the ancient forests and wildlife which belong only in this land.

Of course, in the short space of a television programme we could not hope to tell this complex story. Yet our film about the kokako was entitled "Song of Protest" and the spirit of the forest conservation movement was very much a part of the mood of the programme.

This was possible because during the time we were filming our documentary we heard a song — a song which seemed to catch in its lyrics and melody the whole feeling of the kokako, its cry, the forest in which it lives, and also the human awareness of these things and how they are changing. When we played this song against a counterpoint of the kokako's cries, our film seemed to gain a new meaning. Perhaps this was because the writer, Syd Melbourne, had grown up with an awareness of the "stories and magic" of the forest world characteristic of his Tuhoe tribe — the tribe called by an early anthropologist "Children of the Mist". His song, combined with images of shafts of sunlight and early morning mist in the forest, and the "blue-wattled crow" singing his own song, gave a deeper feeling to the scenes we'd filmed.

Syd Melbourne had written this song because of his own growing concern about the disappearance of the forest and its creatures. This concern had begun because, after talking to Tawhao Tioke, an elder of his tribe, he had come to realise just how important the forest was in Maori culture:

He told me that all the stories and proverbs that arise in Maoridom are lessons learned from nature, because we used to be able to talk to trees, to talk to birds — our people could understand them.

Many traditional Maori stories had grown out of the forest environment — including two about the kokako which Syd told us and which we told in our programmes.

There was the one about the black mask over the bird's face, a story linking it with its extinct relative, the huia:

The kokako was a grey bird, and didn't think it was beautiful enough, so it stole feathers from the huia. It had just taken enough for that black mask over its eyes when it got caught.

Another story told how the bird acquired its beautiful voice — and added new charm to some of the scenes of bird behaviour we had filmed:

The kokako stole its voice from the bag-moth. Our story is that the goddess of flute-music embodied her secret in the bag-moth. So in order to get the heavenly sound of the flute to beautify its own voice, the kokako ate the bag-moth. And now, to keep that sound in its voice it must keep on eating bag-moths — the little flutes hanging from the branches. In this way, the kokako has kept the secret and become the guardian of flute-music for life.

More than this, the forest had been a source of lessons and knowledge about life. For

Kokako scientist working in forest canopy. Photo Rod Hay

instance, Syd said there was the proverb of the whitehead — a little bird which could climb the giant kahikatea, the tallest tree in the forest. This was taken to be telling the people: "You might be small and insignificant but there is a role for you to play. You can achieve great things in spite of physical handicaps."

Important rituals in Maori ceremonies were also learned from the forest. The dance of a man wielding a taiaha with little darting movements during a welcoming ceremony on the marae is derived from the dance of piwakawaka the fantail, who meets strangers coming into the forest with a fluttering, darting challenge, as if to say: "Do you come in peace or war?" The fantail reminds people that they are entering the world of Tane and must do things according to the customs of that world. And so people remind each other of their obligations when entering a strange marae.

Syd Melbourne had come to feel that to have a true understanding of the old wisdom of his people, it was important to have an understanding of the natural world out of which it grew. And he was also concerned that if people were cut off from the natural world of the forest, and lived in an environment just of farms and towns, their imaginations would become impoverished and their wisdom would not grow.

He wanted to help make people aware of the forest world which was disappearing; not through speeches or articles in books, but through song. He began writing songs based on the calls of birds, as his way of trying to keep alive an awareness of the forest world. Some of the songs were simply echoes and variations on the themes of the various bird calls. Others were songs of protest about how the last of the birds' ancient forest was being destroyed, and it was a song like this which we used in our documentary — a song inspired by the drama of events at Pureora:

Te Kokako by Sydney Melbourne

No Tuawhakarere
Rawa mai
I te orokohanga
Rawa mai
Ki te ao marama

Ko te pu ko te kakau
Ko nga peka ko nga rau
Ko nga hua ma nga manu
O te Wao nui a Tane

Patuki ohorere
Taku manawa
Korewa ake nei
Taku kiri e
Mura, mura, mura
O te ahi ka e
Puha auahi
Pungarehu

From beyond the time
Of memory
From the very creation
Of the world of light

Grew the roots, the stem
The branches, the leaves
The fruits for the birds
Of Tane's sacred forest

My heart
startled
My skin
withered
in the flames
of burning fires
choking smoke,
smouldering to ashes

Giant podocarps (matai), Pureora. Photo Rod Hay

Rere ana te konakona
Rere ana te maramara
Wawa wawa
Te Wao a Tane
I te wewe wewe
O te kani mihini
Puha auahi
Poro rakau

Pupu ake
Te aroha
I ahau
Patuki ohorere
Taku manawa
I te porotanga
O te Wao a Tane e
Au i e taukuri

Ka pa mai
he rongo
He manu korowhio
Koro whiti, koro whiti
whio, whio, whiu

Te kokako
E ko nei
I te marama
I te po
Ki te tupua
Ki a Tane

Tukua iho
To korowai
To atawhai
To manakai
Hei maru
mo to manu
E ko nei

Kati te tuatua noa
I nga taonga
i waihotia mai
Hei atawhai
He manaki
Ma tatua
mo nga reanga

Chips and pieces fly
The forest of Tane
resounds with the noise
of mechanical saws
bellowing smoke
hacking trees

My emotions
well up
My heart beats with
panic at the
destruction of Tane's
domain

A sound is heard
A song bird
Koro whiti
Koro whiti
whio, whio, whiu

Kokako
making a plea
in the morning in the
evening
to the ancestor
Tane the protector

Let down
Your cloak
Your embrace
Your blessing
to protect your
bird
pleading to you

Cease this careless
destruction of the
treasures that were
left to us to safeguard
and cherish for
those yet to be born.

Mist over the forest at dawn, Oparara Valley. Photo Guy Salmon

The words of this song tell of anger and distress. The melody, echoing the kokako's song, is full of sadness and longing for the disappearing forest. By combining the song with our images of the kokako, we hoped that our programme "Song of Protest" would say to people what Syd Melbourne had also said:

The song of the kokako has become the voice of the forest. The call is now to the people. The kokako cries out: "Many birds suffered for the use of mankind. Your survival once depended on us. Now our survival depends on you. What are you going to do?" That is the challenge.

Will we have the imagination to meet that challenge or will our ancient extraordinary birds only be fully appreciated after they have been silenced forever?

Foreword

Supplement to the Birds of New Zealand W. L. Buller, published by the Author, London 1905
"The Lighthouse Keeper's Cat" Rod Morris in **School Journal** Part One Number Two, New Zealand Department of Education 1980

Chapter One
Beginnings

New Zealand Adrift G. R. Stevens, AH & AW Reed, Wellington 1980
The Geological History of New Zealand and its Life C. A. Fleming, Auckland University Press and Oxford University Press, Auckland 1979
"The Coming of the Birds" C. A. Fleming in **New Zealand's Nature Heritage** 3:61–68, Hamlyns Ltd, Hong Kong 1974
"Systematics of the New Zealand short-tailed bat *Mystacina*, Gray 1843 (*Chiroptera: Mystacinidae*)" J. E. Hill and M. J. Daniel in **Bulletin of British Museum of Natural History (Zoology)** 48: Number 4, London 1985
The Tuatara, Lizards and Frogs of New Zealand Richard Sharell, Collins, Auckland 1966
Rails of the World S. Dillon Ripley, David R. Codine, Boston 1977
"The Laughing Owl (*Sceloglaux albifacies*)" M. H. Douglas in **Review 39: Journal of the Tussock Grasslands & Mountain Lands Institute,** Christchurch 1980
"The Affinities of the New Zealand passerine Genus *Turnagra*" S. L. Olson, K. C. Parkes, M. H. Cleuch and S. R. Borecky in ***Notornis*** 31:273–277 (1984)
The Naturalization of plants and animals in New Zealand G. M. Thomson, Cambridge University Press, Cambridge 1922
"The Status of Endangered New Zealand Birds" J. A. Mills and G. R. Williams in **The Status of Endangered Australasian Wildlife** The Royal Zoological Society of South Australia 1978

Chapter Two
Brief Encounters

Huia:
A History of the Birds of New Zealand W. L. Buller, published by the Author, London 1888 (Second edition)
Travels in New Zealand E. Dieffenbach, J. Murray, London 1843
The Book of the Huia W. J. Phillips, Whitcombe & Tombs, Christchurch 1963

Moa:
The moa-hunter period of Maori culture R. Duff, Government Printer, Wellington 1977 (Third edition)
The Moa, when did it become extinct? Herries Beattie, published by the Author, no date [1940's]
When all the moa ovens grew cold Athol Anderson, Otago Heritage Books, Dunedin 1983
"Evolution of Divaricating plants in New Zealand in relation to Moa browsing" R. M. Greenwood and I. A. E. Atkinson in **Proceedings of New Zealand Ecological Society** Volume 24:21–33 (1977)
Pioneers of Martins Bay Alice McKenzie, Whitcombe & Tombs 1952 (Revised edition)

Kiwi:
"Incubation temperatures of the North Island Brown Kiwi *Apteryx australis mantelli*" Barry Rowe in ***Notornis*** 25:213–217 (1978)
"The Kiwi" William Calder III in **Scientific American**, July 1978
"Of Kiwi Eggs and the Liberty Bell" Stephen Jay Gould in **Natural History**, New York, November 1986
"The Birth of a Kiwi" Barry Rowe & Rod Morris in **School Journal** Part Two Number Three, 1981
Forest Lore of the Maori Elsdon Best, Government Printer, Wellington 1942 (Reprinted 1977)

Kea:
Pioneer work in the Alps of New Zealand A. P. Harper, T. Fisher Unwin, London 1896
A Kea on my Bed Molly Falla, Collins, Auckland 1974
The Kea: A New Zealand Problem G. R. Marriner, Marriner Bros. & Co., Christchurch 1908
A History of the Birds of New Zealand W. L. Buller published by the Author, London 1888 (Second edition)
Beak of the Moon Philip Temple, Collins, Auckland 1981

Chapter Three
Takahe

A History of the Birds of New Zealand W. L. Buller, published by the Author, London 1888 (Second edition)
"The Bird that Hid" G. B. Orbell in **School Journal** Part Three Number Three 1986
"Population studies on takahe (*Notornis mantelli*) in Fiordland" J. A. Mills in **XII Bulletin of International Council for Bird Preservation,** Cambridge 1975
"Red deer as a factor in the decline of takahe numbers" J. A. Mills in **Seminar on Science in National Parks** National Parks Authority, Wellington 1977
"Food preferences of takahe in Fiordland National Park, New Zealand, and the effect of competition from introduced red deer" J. A. Mills & A. F. Mark in **Journal of Animal Ecology** 46:939–958 (1977)
"Population studies of takahe" J. A. Mills in **Seminar on the takahe and its habitat,** Fiordland National Parks Board, Invercargill 1978
"Captive Rearing of Takahe" Craig Robertson in **Forest & Bird** November 1986

Chapter Four
Black Stilt

High Endeavour: History of the Mackenzie Country William Vance, published by the Author, Timaru 1965

A comparative ecological study of pied and black stilts in South Canterbury R. J. Pierce, Unpublished Ph.D. dissertation, University of Otago, Dunedin 1982

"The black stilt: endangered bird of the high country" R. J. Pierce in **Forest & Bird,** August 1980

"A record breeding season for the black stilts in the wild" R. J. Pierce in **Forest & Bird,** May 1983

"Plumage, morphology and hybridisation of New Zealand stilts *(Himantopus spp.)*" R. J. Pierce in ***Notornis*** 31:106–130 (1984)

"The changed distribution of stilts in New Zealand" R. J. Pierce in ***Notornis*** 31:7–18 (1984)

"Foraging responses of stilts *(Himantopus spp.)* to changes in abundance and behaviour of their riverbed prey" R. J. Pierce in **N.Z. Journal of Marine and Freshwater Research** 20:17–28 (1986)

"Feeding methods of stilts *(Himantopus spp.)*" R. J. Pierce in **N.Z. Journal of Zoology** 12:467–472 (1985)

"Differences in susceptibility to predation during nesting between pied and black stilts *(Himantopus spp.)*" R. J. Pierce in **Auk** 103:273–280 (1986)

Chapter Five
Saddleback

Out in the Open T. H. Potts, Lyttelton Times, Christchurch 1870

Yesterdays in Maoriland A. Reischek, translated by H. E. L. Priday, Jonathan Cape, London 1930

Children of Tane Mona Gordon, Whitcombe & Tombs, Christchurch 1938

"Spread of the ship rat *(Rattus rattus L.)* in New Zealand" I. A. E. Atkinson in **Journal of the Royal Society of New Zealand** Vol. 3 No. 3: 457–472 (1973)

"The Big South Cape Islands rat irruption" B. D. Bell in **The ecology and control of rodents in New Zealand nature reserves** edited by P. R. Dingwall, I. A. E. Atkinson, and C. Hay, Dept. of Lands and Survey Information Series 4, 1978

"A Century of Change within the New Zealand Forest" I. A. E. Atkinson in **Forest & Bird,** August 1973

"Evidence for the effects of rodents on the vertebrate wildlife of New Zealand islands" I. A. E. Atkinson in **The ecology and control of rodents in New Zealand nature reserves** edited by P. R. Dingwall, I. A. E. Atkinson and C. Hay, Dept. of Lands and Survey Information Series 4 1978

"New Zealand's Unique Burrowing Bats are Endangered" Mike Daniel in **Bats** Newsletter of Bat Conservation International Vol 2 Number 3, Milwaukee 1985

"Controlling introduced predators and competitors on islands" D. V. Merton in **Endangered Birds** edited by S. A. Temple, Croom Helm, London 1978

"The saddleback: its status and conservation" D. V. Merton in **Breeding Endangered Species in Captivity** edited by R. D. Martin, Academic Press, London & New York 1975

"Success in re-establishing a threatened species: the saddleback — its status and conservation". D. V. Merton in **XII Bulletin of International Council for Bird Preservation** Cambridge 1975

Red Data Book (Vol 2 Aves) published by International Union for Conservation of Nature and Natural Resources, Morges, Switzerland 1979.

Chapter Six
Kakapo

Children of Tane Mona Gordon, Whitcombe & Tombs, Christchurch 1938

A History of the Birds of New Zealand W. L. Buller, published by the Author, London 1888 (Second edition)

The habits of the flightless birds of New Zealand Richard Henry, Government Printer, Wellington 1903

Forest Lore of the Maori Elsdon Best, Government Printer, Wellington 1942 (Reprinted 1977)

"The kakapo's secret" Rod Morris in **School Journal** Part One Number One 1977

"Lek behaviour in a parrot: the kakapo *(Strigops habroptilus)* of New Zealand" D. V. Merton, R. B. Morris, and I. A. E. Atkinson in **Ibis** Journal of the British Ornithologists' Union 126 Number three 1984

Chapter Seven
Black Robin

"The Chatham Island black robin, extinction or survival?" J. A. D. Flack in **XII Bulletin of International Council for Bird Preservation,** Cambridge 1975

"Black Robin transfers" R. B. Morris in **Wildlife — a Review** Number 8 NZ Wildlife Service, Wellington 1977

"Seven Black Robins" Rod Morris in **School Journal** Part Three Number One 1980

"The plight of the black robin in the Chathams" Rod Morris in **Forest & Bird** February 1981

"Robin capable of full recovery on Mangere Island" D. V. Merton in **Forest & Bird** February 1981

Chapter Eight
Yellow-eyed Penguin

Camera Studies of New Zealand Birds (Series B) No. 6 L. E. Richdale, published by the Author, Dunedin, no date [1945]

"Pair-formation in Penguins" L. E. Richdale in **Emu** 46, Melbourne 1946

A study of a group of penguins of known age (Biological Monographs 1) L. E. Richdale published by the Author, Dunedin 1949

Sexual Behaviour in Penguins L. E. Richdale, University of

Kansas Press, Lawrence 1951
A Population Study of Penguins L. E. Richdale, Oxford University Press, London 1957
Podgy the Penguin (Bird Books for Children No. 1) L. E. Richdale, published by the Author, Dunedin, no date [1947]
"Obituary for Lancelot Eric Richdale O.B.E., M.A., D.Sc, (NZ), F.L.S., Hectors Medalist, 1900–1983" by C. A. Fleming in **Proceedings of the Royal Society of New Zealand** 112 (1984)
"Proof is the Authority" Christopher Robertson in **NZ Listener** March 1986
Draft Species Recovery Plan for the Yellow-eyed Penguin (Megadyptes antipodes) published by the NZ Wildlife Service, Dunedin 1986
"A royal albatross nesting on the Otago Peninsula, New Zealand" L. E. Richdale in **Emu** 38, Melbourne 1939
"The starvation theory in albatrosses" L. E. Richdale in **Auk** 71, Washington 1954
The royal albatross (Diomedea epomophora sanfordi) (Series A) No 2 L. E. Richdale, published by the Author, Dunedin 1942

Chapter Nine
Kokako

The Forest World of New Zealand J. H. Johns and C. G. R. Chavasse, AH & AW Reed, Wellington 1975
"The Kokako, perspective and prospect" Rod Hay in **Forest & Bird,** February 1984
"The Influence of browsing by introduced mammals on the decline of the North Island kokako" J. R. Leathwick, J. R. Hay and A. E. Fitzgerald in **NZ Journal of Ecology** 6:55–70 (1983)
Distribution and habitats of native bird species in indigenous state forests of the Rotorua and Taupo districts I. G. Crook, D. V. Merton and L. R. Moran, unpublished report, Wildlife Service, Wellington 1971
"Pureora Forest Park — a haven of the kokako" an article contributed by the Forest Service in **Forest & Bird** August 1981
"Pureora Forest Park — the conservation view" Alan Edmonds in **Forest & Bird** February 1982
The kokako and Central North Island rain forests C. A. Fleming, an address given to ECO Conference, May 1977
"Regeneration of podocarps in a Central North Island forest" A. E. Beveridge in **NZ Journal of Forestry** 73:23–25, 1973
"What future for kauri?" Mark Bellingham in **Forest & Bird,** August 1984
To Save a Forest — Whirinaki J. Morton, J. Ogden, T. Hughes, The Whirinaki Forest Promotion Trust, Auckland 1984
